Thinking in Icons

Dedicated to my sun, moon, and stars, Brooke, Natalie, and Skylar

Inspiring | Educating | Creating | Entertaining

Brimming with creative inspiration, how-to projects, and useful information to enrich your everyday life, Quarto Knows is a favorite destination for those pursuing their interests and passions. Visit our site and dig deeper with our books into your area of interest: Quarto Creates, Quarto Cooks, Quarto Homes, Quarto Lives, Quarto Drives, Quarto Explores, Quarto Gifts, or Quarto Kids.

First Published in 2017 by Rockport Publishers, an imprint of The Quarto Group, 100 Cummings Center, Suite 265-D, Beverly, MA 01915, USA.
T (978) 282-9590 F (978) 283-2742 QuartoKnows.com

Rockport Publishers titles are also available at discount for retail, wholesale, promotional, and bulk purchase. For details, contact the Special Sales Manager by email at specialsales@quarto.com or by mail at The Quarto Group, Attn: Special Sales Manager, 401 Second Avenue North, Suite 310, Minneapolis, MN 55401, USA.

10 9 8 7 6 5 4 3 2 1

ISBN: 978-1-63159-314-7

Digital edition published in 2017

Library of Congress Cataloging-in-Publication Data available

Design, cover image, and page layout: Landers Miller Design
Photography: James Worrell
Illustration: Felix Sockwell

Printed in China

Thinking in Icons

Designing and creating effective visual symbols

Felix Sockwell
with Emily Potts
Foreword by Steven Heller

ROCKPORT

Contents

7 **Foreword by Steven Heller**

11 **Introduction**

15 Icons for **Interactive**
032 Bill Gardner

35 Icons for **Branding**

113 Icons for **Editorial**
114 John Korpics
124 Brian Rea

137 Icons for **Wayfinding**

156 **About the Authors**

157 **Index**

The Language of Icons

Steven Heller

The random vocalizing of speechlike syllables seemingly devoid of logical meaning is called "speaking in tongues." The textual equivalent, "automatic writing," is when words and sentences that do not consciously come from the actual writer spring forth on a page. These are fascinating concepts to ponder, and while there is no direct correlation between speaking in tongues or automatic writing with *Thinking in Icons*, there are some notable similarities.

Icons: Otto Neurath

In fact, think of this introduction, indeed the book itself, as a channeling of icon designers from past and present who understand that pictorial representations were and are essential to linguistics—and often easier to comprehend. Icons are not only a truly universal language, but they also provide nuances that might be lost on the printed word. Remember the old adage: A picture is worth . . . .

Writing began as a visual experience, either as representational drawings on prehistoric cave walls or inscribed marks on ancient stone or wood, invested either with symbolic meanings or phonetic attributes. It is no surprise that icons long ago were used to present ideas in all manner of public and private messaging, large and small. Today, a yellow sign showing a running child with a ball is more easily and quickly "read" than simply writing "children at play."

It is impossible to teach language without using pictures. What's more, many of the world's contemporary writing systems are not alphabetic but logographic and ideographic, representing objects and ideas, rather than sounds of words. Of course, actual letters can be designed to exude verbal expression as the Italian Futurists did with onomatopoeia, by changing the size, shape, and juxtaposition of letters and words to simulate sound in type. Graphic design was largely invented as an amalgam of these systems. For centuries, the language of graphic design has been a fundamental interplay of word and picture, while over the past thirty or so years, sound and motion have become more essential. Maybe the next big revolution will be telepathy—but that's another book (or thought).

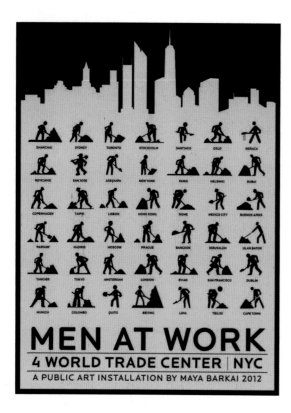

In the realm of type, a few twentieth-century progressive type designers, Lucian Bernhard and Bradbury Thompson among them, attempted to make learning English easier by altering and simplifying the Latin alphabet. Twenty-six letters should not be that difficult to decipher, but the distinction between caps and lowercase, as well as confusing letter juxtapositions, can be chaotic. With icons, recognizing pictographs and ideograms is faster and possibly more precise.

The confluence of the computer and information ages from the 1980s to now has increased the need for abbreviated language. Emojis are useful, are impossible to ignore, and represent an increasing reliance on imagery to express—at least superficially—human thought and deed. But even earlier, many people used the abstract heart image to say "I love you" long before Milton Glaser's I ♥ NY logo was released. The reason for its popularity and longevity is the result of its incredible utility and familiarity. Icons are functional but also personable. Like typefaces, there are many varieties saying the same thing, stylistically made to have differing impacts on readers.

This is a book of images used in the same manner as type—not as typefaces per se, but they are surrogates for words and phrases. Each works particularly well for the job it is meant to do. Just as sans serif type impacts a reader's perception and comprehension differently than serif type does, a lightline icon will have a different impact than the bolder iteration. Each type of icon speaks to a unique part of the conscious and subconscious. In this sense, designers who use them are speaking in icons that have specific meanings.

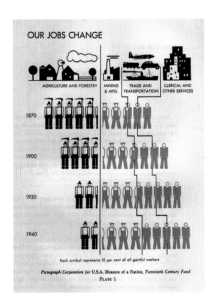

How Icons Have Been Used Throughout History
Men at Work poster, Maya Barkai,
2012 (opposite top)

I ♥ NY logo, Milton Glaser, 1977 (opposite middle)

Infographic symbols, AIGA committee members: Thomas Geismar, Seymour Chwast, Rudolph de Harak, John Lees, Massimo Vignelli; Designers: Roger Cook and Don Shanosky, 1972 (along bottom, both pages)

Tokyo Olympics, Katsumi Masaru, 1964 (top)

Our Jobs Change, Otto Neurath, 1945 (bottom)

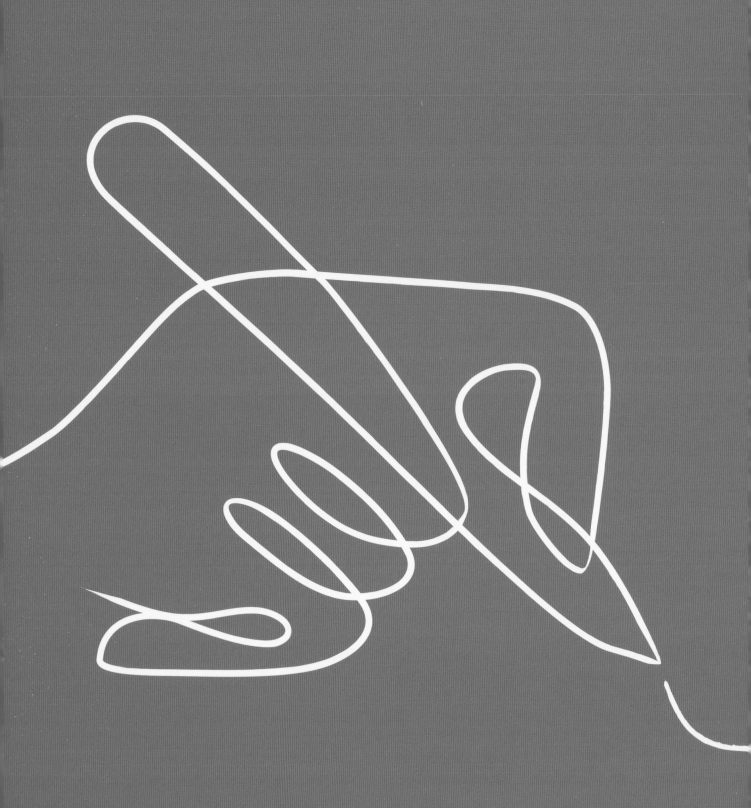

Introduction

What is an icon? For me, it's anything, really: a color, symbol, pictogram, emoji, button, logo, isotope, or wayfinding visual—anything that represents an idea or a picture. Icons deliver information and instruction for medicine, travel, and brands; they can do anything you tell them to do (or vice versa). Icons help you find the restroom, identify your favorite brands, or guide you on your next adventure. This book unveils the mystery and magic of icons through form and function, art and science, and attempts to bridge the gaps we've missed in the future of short-form, cryptic communication.

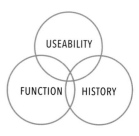

Long-form communication, in recent years, has given way to the short form. Words are losing power to the useful shorthand that icons (or emojis) deliver. In the future, imagine a new language—one that isn't Portuguese, English, or Spanish; imagine conversations in icons.

Usability, Function, History
The history informs the usability and the function. Meanings evolve over time, which can change the perception and function of an icon if it doesn't also evolve.

Icons, like art, are what you can get away with. Aside from illustrating the creative process of icons, we'll also highlight new uses and applications for consideration—animation, sculpture, signage, and art—and how each discipline affects how we come to better understand them and ourselves.

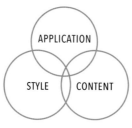

Style, Application, Content
Style and content need to work toward the application in order for an icon to effectively deliver its message.

Iconography, for me, functions in a way similar to sans serif letterforms: icons are a quick expression, distilled, and universally received. They're not fussy. They're also entertainment. Emojis, a recent phenomenon in texting, are shorthand for a broad range of emotions and general sentiments. Even our abbreviated language—LOL, OMG, LMAO—is slowly being replaced with icons. No one has time to type. Who knows? Maybe the future keyboard will include the poop emoji.

We'll discuss the art of negotiation and compromise and the frustrations endured being an artist in an overlooked art. People don't consider the art of icons until the icons aren't working and they're lost, frustrated, and confused. For instance, wayfinding icons work best when they seamlessly blend into the landscape and inform the user where to go or what to do. The message is simple and instantly understood in any language.

"People don't consider the art of icons until they're frustrated and confused."

Part of the joy of creating pictures is storytelling, immersing your audience in something without them knowing what's happening—seduction, trickery—alongside the familiar. This is what great brands do and why we develop bonds with brands and become loyal followers.

Brands can't connect and separate themselves unless they're different, and often, a simple icon does that. Think of all the brands you see on a daily basis and the one defining element is the logo. Many logos are icons that have been around for years. Think Red Cross, Apple, NBC, Girl Scouts, Playboy, and Starbucks. In this book, we look at several brands and the icons I worked up.

My emotive insertion into the art of icon design came early—in college. I was tasked with coming up with a poster to encourage theatergoers to buy season tickets to the school's annual plays. I had no idea what I was doing, but I felt like designating the spaces with appropriate imagery would endear and inform. The theater had never employed a designer. Their full breadth of promotional materials was an 8.5 x 11-inch (21.5 × 28 cm) sheet of paper folded in half with a list of shows and a subscription form.

By the end of the school year, my little accordion-fold poster (that functioned as a mailer and brochure) had been reprinted four times, and the theater had gone from 40 percent attendance to full capacity. If that weren't enough, one day as I was eating a burger at a local dive, a waitress—tipped off by one of the cooks—approached my table. She asked, "Are you the designer of the colorful poster with all the icons?" I was caught off guard. "Yes," I replied. She said, "I wanted to tell you how much that poster meant to me. My parents were able to see me perform in front a full house, and I think I may be going to New York soon!" I didn't know quite what to say but she took my hand, came in closer, and a slow smile crept into her tearful gaze. "You changed my life. Thank you."

Ninety percent of the work shown within these pages is completely fake—drawn up in the sidebars of actual assignments. Some of them are redrafted explorations, staged buffoonery cloaked in optimism. I've experienced just about every high and low in my twenty-five years spent vectoring icons. If I told you how it really went down, you'd never go to art school.

"Interactive icons should be so simple that they are invisible to users."

Interactive

16 *New York Times*
       app icons for the iPhone
20 iTunes
24 Yahoo!
26 AT&T
28 Amplify

Most solutions to interactive problems are built on an existing lexicon: what symbols already communicate. For instance, a shopping cart usually denotes a purchasing function, while some retailers may use a dollar sign. Of course, if the business is international, a dollar sign wouldn't work. There are so many factors to consider when designing an icon that it often takes teams of people and testing to make sure the right visual language is built for its intended purpose. People rely on their devices for information in a hurry, so keeping the icons simple (often colorless) eases the mind's eye and communicates faster. They should be so simple and easy to read that there's no thought whatsoever about the design. When they're not noted or fussed with, their utility is being served. Icons that are deliberately "design-y" or "fun" for aesthetic reasons become dated in the long run. Interactive icons are all about getting users from point A to point B in the shortest amount of time possible, without them having to think about what they're looking at.

New York Times app icons for the iPhone

Pioneering new territory with a smart system of icons for the leader in news

CLIENT
New York Times

ART DIRECTORS
Carolyn Tutino
Khoi Vinh

Shortly after the first iPhone was released in 2007, *New York Times* art directors Khoi Vinh and Carolyn Tutino hired me to create icons for each section of the paper for the new NYT app. It was one of the first editorial apps, so it was all new territory for me. The intent of these icons, more than any other in this book, was to be invisible, stay out of the way, and not get noticed. The effect, then, is that you read the icons like information, not styled art. They're for when you need to get somewhere and get there fast.

Here are some rules that applied to this project:

- One image per category
- No gradients (aside from the *Times Magazine*)
- Simple and readable in all languages
- Equal distribution of distinguished shapes (squares to circles to triangles)
- Fast read

What's fascinating to me—revelatory, even—is how the public grasps certain images and tosses away others. Let's take the Tulip icon, for example: thirteen years ago, before the iPhone, this icon was widely seen on the Canon camera and other common devices. It meant picture, or more accurately, still life. I initially designed a tombstone for the Obituaries section, but no one wants to be reminded of his or her dead Uncle Harry—it's too morbid. Ironically, they decided to go with a Tulip. It sort of boggles the mind how a skull can't represent death. People can't handle the truth. People die. And most of the time, especially in foreign countries, you don't go out and buy tulips. You get cremated.

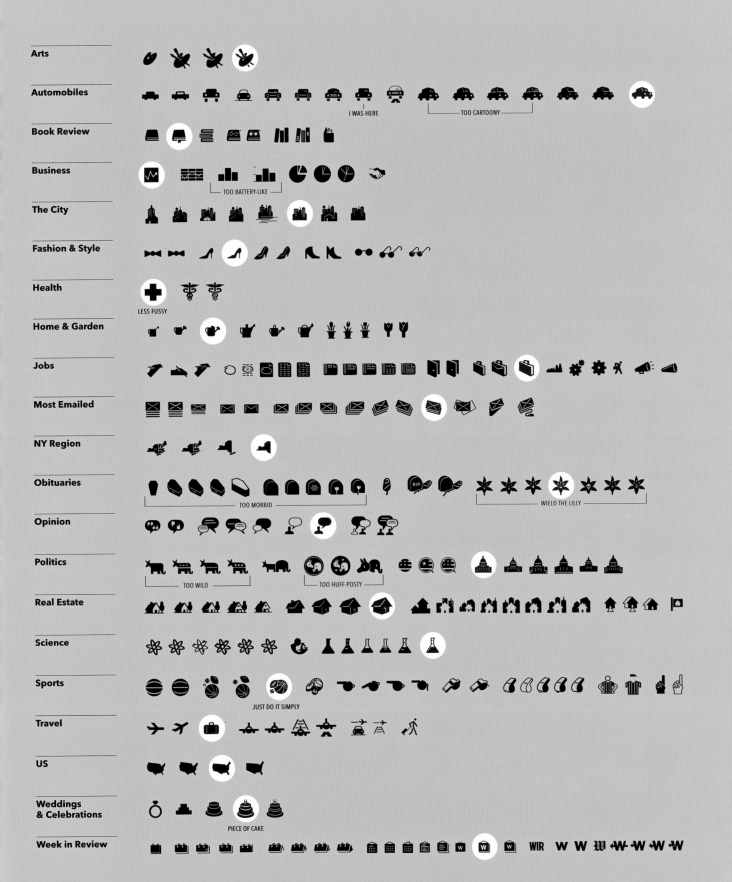

Arts

Automobiles
I WAS HERE TOO CARTOONY

Book Review

Business
TOO BATTERY-LIKE

The City

Fashion & Style

Health
LESS FUSSY

Home & Garden

Jobs

Most Emailed

NY Region

Obituaries
TOO MORBID WIELD THE LILLY

Opinion

Politics
TOO WILD TOO HUFF-POSTY

Real Estate

Science

Sports
JUST DO IT SIMPLY

Travel

US

Weddings & Celebrations
PIECE OF CAKE

Week in Review
WIR

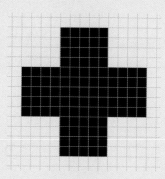

32 Pixels
If the design doesn't work in black and white in 32 pixels, you're screwed.

Dimensional vs. Flat
In the initial design, we had slight dimensional qualities in some of the icons, but these were later flattened for consistency.

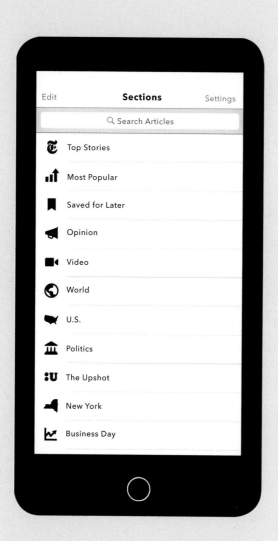

Edit	**Sections**	Settings

🔍 Search Articles

Top Stories

Most Popular

Saved for Later

Opinion

Video

World

U.S.

Politics

The Upshot

New York

Business Day

New York Times **app**

Line Weight
A similar line weight was used throughout the series.

Complete Set First Release

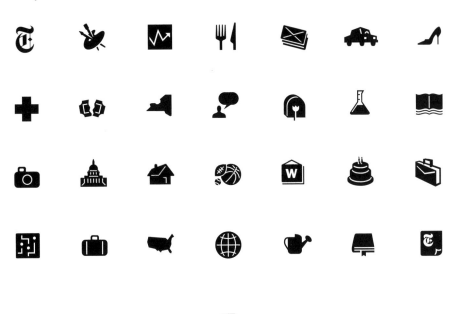

Revised Set

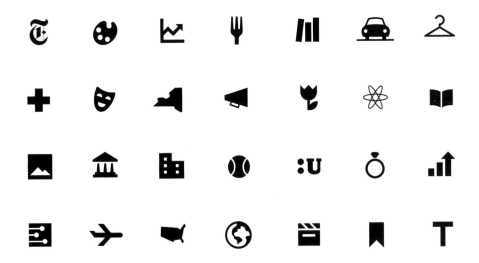

Evolution of a System
As you can see, some icons changed little, while others were completely transformed over time. Most of the changes are for the better—they are simpler and much easier to cognitively translate.

Sport is a tough one to crack, with so many different sports to cover, so this icon was the most complicated. I initially gave them a few different options, and they ended up using a referee shirt in the first iteration. That was later changed to a generic ball. I guess over time, people have gotten used to the idea of the icon looking like a tennis ball. I went in and thinned the lines so it's more of a generic-looking ball.

I knew that whatever we did had to be blocky and thick. I took shapes and paired them together. I did the same thing with the house and the car. We drew them really small to see how they would look on a phone screen. This hadn't been done before, so we were learning as we went along. Over time, they changed them and improved upon them.

You don't want to get confused or introduced with a new visual parlance. Change happens slowly. This system slowly improved over time. I've updated and changed some of the icons over the years, including the latest set, shown here.

iTunes

Taking notes in circles

CLIENT
Apple

ART DIRECTOR
Jeff Zwerner

Everyone recognizes the iTunes icon—it's pretty brilliant in its simplicity. And no, I didn't do it, though I tried. I was hired in 2004 to update it, but all of my ideas missed the mark. I was trying too hard to come up with something different, and then they ended up using a nonproprietary mark—a music note in a circle. They're not selling or promoting anything, so it works. The best, most effective work, in this regard, is work, or information, that doesn't stand out or get noticed. Its function is to show you where music is. I failed miserably—the bloggers were right.

History of the iTunes Note Icon

Joel
"This is a disgrace. How the HELL did this guy get the opportunity to even present these to Steve when they are this horrid? This man has no sense of design!"

Aaron
"Apparently this guy doesn't know that the 'OK' hand symbol means 'a--hole' in other countries . . . "

twitter-19413173
"What the hell, was he drunk coming up with these?"

iTunes v4 2003   iTunes v7 2007   iTunes v11 2011

I had no idea this gesture meant a—hole in thirteen countries.

There really aren't any good ideas here.

I often show a linear icon scrawl to make it look like I did more work.

Yahoo!

Making the rounds

There wasn't a set aesthetic to flesh out. We just started distilling the information as best we could. These are also pre-retina high-resolution displays, so we were aiming for less dimensional icons, which looked dated on traditional screens.

CLIENT
Ogilvy & Mather

CREATIVE DIRECTOR
Sung Chang

ART DIRECTOR
Barbara Glauber

Yahoo! hired Ogilvy to do a massive redesign for its website around 2003. At the time, Yahoo! was the biggest player on the Internet. Yahoo! wanted to shift away from the little yellow emojis of the fun face. They were kind of hokey. There were six divisions or ideas to illustrate, so I toyed with multiple concepts for each. Talk about tweaking something to death. How

many different ways can you draw an envelope? Apparently, thirty-four! Move it this way, turn it that way, or put a blue circle behind it.

Yahoo! didn't use my work in the end, but I sold some of the scraps to AT&T, so it wasn't a total loss.

My Yahoo!

Each house was purposely set to come out of the circle to create an entry point. It's also about using the space judiciously.

Finance

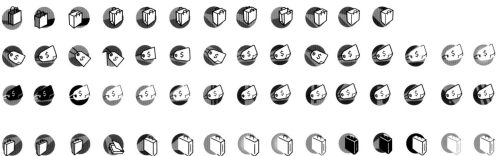

Shopping

Jobs

This icon wouldn't even make sense anymore. In the early days of the Internet, the briefcase was associated with careers, but people don't make that association anymore. It's an antiquated image.

Messenger

Messaging was big when Yahoo! first came on the scene, and a lot of that pinging was young love, which is why there are so many hearts.

Email

AT&T

They bought the house that Yahoo! passed on

CLIENT
Interbrand

ART DIRECTOR
Craig Stout

One of the most powerful, effective, and copied trademarks of all time is the AT&T "Death Star" mark designed by Saul Bass's team, under the leadership of Jerry "the King" Kuyper—a collaborator on the initial 2006 *New York Times* Science Times icons (page 146).

The public doesn't realize how much research, rigor, and design go into marks such as these, and the comments are usually knee-jerk ("looks like a five-year-old did it") once the work is launched. Craig Stout, a neighbor of mine, helped usher in the new 3-D icon, which, for all intents and purposes, works quite well. In building out a set of print icons for Craig, we went about it in the usual way—by borrowing from work that preceded it, notably the stuff I worked up for Yahoo! (on the previous spread).

Original Stylistic Directions

Info-graffyk
These were rejects from Liberty Mutual Insurance in 2002. I usually show a smattering of styles to get consensus on direction before moving forward.

Tekky
This is what computer graphic icons looked like in 1999. Scary.

Original Logo
Saul Bass, 1986

Redesigned Logo
Interbrand, 2005

Amorphic
These fall into a kind of science category.

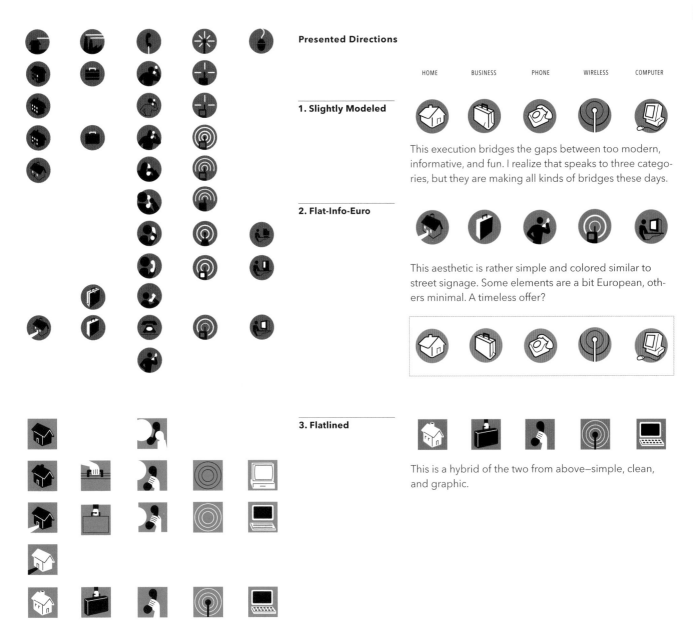

Presented Directions

	HOME	BUSINESS	PHONE	WIRELESS	COMPUTER

1. Slightly Modeled

This execution bridges the gaps between too modern, informative, and fun. I realize that speaks to three categories, but they are making all kinds of bridges these days.

2. Flat-Info-Euro

This aesthetic is rather simple and colored similar to street signage. Some elements are a bit European, others minimal. A timeless offer?

3. Flatlined

This is a hybrid of the two from above—simple, clean, and graphic.

4. Amorphic

Here we have an older style coming back to life. There is plenty of personality and ownability. It's worth showing if more style is on the brief.

5. Linear

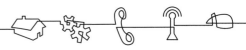

Because this direction was nearly complete, I went ahead and knocked it all out.

Amplify

Learning two and three sums

CLIENT
Co-collective (Co:)

ART DIRECTORS
Ty Montague
Graham Clifford

Amplify is an online educational resource for teachers and students in grades K through 8. They provide hardware, software, and curriculum for schools. The trick for this trifecta was trying to decide how to separate and unite the three divisions of the company. Usually, when you present an icon that has multiple layers, it's best to stick with two visual ideas so as not to muddy the message. In this case, we ended up merging three ideas to communicate Amplify's educational goals: hand (learning), apple (education), and tree (growth). I typically wouldn't do this, but the double take, tripled, worked. Then, we built out the process for "access" and "insight."

Combining Insight, Learning, and Access

Brand Attributes

OPTIMISTIC

INVENTIVE

THOUGHTFUL

PRACTICAL

TRANSFORMATIVE

ACCESSIBLE

EFFECTIVE

General

INSIGHT

LEARNING

ACCESS

Product

SERVICES

VIEWPOINT

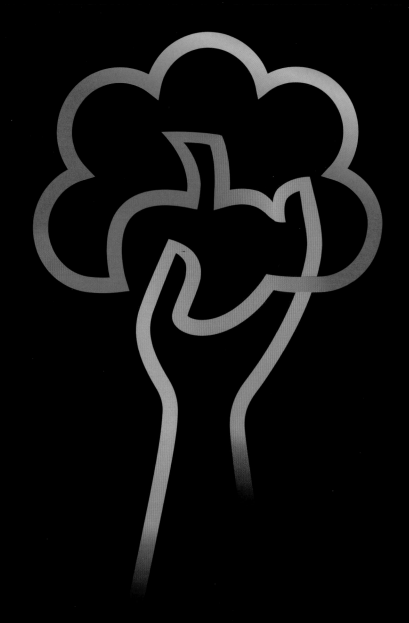

I like to think that an
icon can work as a logo
and a poster, if you're
lucky. For the learning
icon, we took literal and
metaphorical concepts
and combined them
into a simple, layered
puzzle. The various
symbols were applied
to Amplify's site and
devices at appropriate
sizes.

These shorthand symbols were intended to be used in the tablet's interface.

Just a very slight tweak to a standard icon can inform and steer users to clarity. You can over- or underdo it. So we tried three applications: slightly linear (no loops), geometric lines, and a solid fill. The client passed on everything and I ended up refurbing the scrap for a future assignment for Verizon and Michael Bierut's team (which also died).

The Changing Landscape of Icons

Bill Gardner, founder of LogoLounge and Gardner Design

As designers, we all like to think that we are original and the work we create is our own. We're all trying to push things forward and do something that another designer has never done. Anything you design has to have some context, some familiarity, so people know what service or product you're referencing. Any time something is introduced as new, it still has to have some semblance of the past worked into it. It's one of the reasons we rely so much on cliché imagery—because it works. The obligation is to present the cliché in a new and engaging way.

If we're designing something that has to do with Wi-Fi or the broadcast of sound, the most common visual device is a vibrating image or those little rainbow stripes that radiate out. That's not a new concept. This visual language came out of early cartoons. Little lines would be coming out of a ringing phone, indicating to viewers that sound was coming out. It goes far back, and it works now because it was a cliché invented years before. That's how people relate to it.

Symbols, or icons, do this very well, and when they're used as part of a logo, they don't do anything more than serve as a representation of a concept. That's it. We're representing a company's promise and the quality of their products and services.

That's what a logo is: it's a vessel that represents something. However, the vessel is changing. Anything can start to represent something. Color is certainly important. What does the Tiffany logo look like? Does it matter? As long as you see that Tiffany blue, you know what it is. Identities are moving beyond these simple little icons.

That being said, nothing beats a wonderful little icon. It's compact and quickly delivers that message in a little space. By being able to reduce that complete essence down into a symbol, we've managed to maximize the potential of a visual brand because we've minimized the space it takes to convey all of those connotations.

Now we've got favicons (shortcut icons), which are 16 x 16 pixels. That's a teeny tiny space, but it is one of the areas that is most prolific on any digital device. It's a symbol. Sometimes, it can be something other than the logo. Take Google, for instance. There have probably been many favicon variations over the years for Google, and it's not the logo—currently it's the G. But, if you were to show the Google favicon to people and ask what it is, they would probably say that's the Google logo.

Suddenly, you're allowing the environment to control design, and it *should* control design, and it *does* control design. Form does follow function. As designers, we have to realize that the environment that we're designing for is

a changing function, and as our function changes, our form has to adjust to what's going on there.

Even the creative tools we use on the computer were originally created to replicate the analog tools we use—pencil, pen, brush, etc. When an icon was designed on the computer, it was designed with the things that predate it. Now, when you talk to someone about drawing something on the computer, they're using tools that allow points to fractalize, laying down beautiful gradients or multiple layers at once. There's a generation of designers who have never known what it's like to design without the computer. They're laying things down in a much more comprehensive and complex fashion than previous generations imagined.

There was a time when we would say to designers: Draw your ideas, don't use the computer to draw things—it has no soul, no context. That's not true any longer. There are designers who can go straight to the screen and do a great job because that's their environment. Nowadays, it's not even a conversation as to where designers start their work.

That shift in technology meant we could deliver products we couldn't deliver before. You start thinking about the whole idea of print. It's not king anymore. Designers once talked to companies about identity development and what they'd need such as letterhead, business cards, and envelopes. Now, it's just a website and/or an app. So many companies only live in a digital environment.

Our core objective as identity designers is still going to be to transmit the essence of something to somebody symbolically. That's the core of this. That's our job.

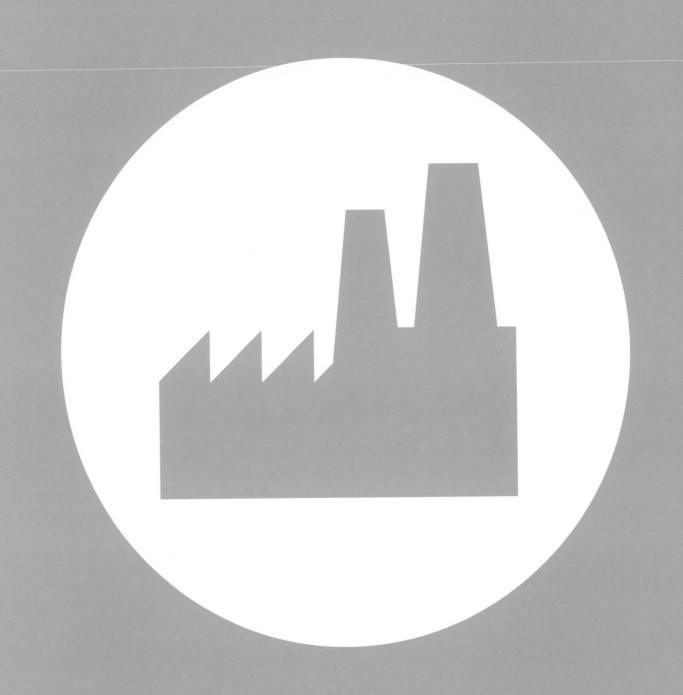

"The icon should be representative of the company's values and commitment to its customers and be easily recognizable."

Branding

36   National Quality
      Center Logo
38   Monopoly Makeover
40   Liberty Mutual
46   Zynga
50   Yogurt Company
52   Apple
54   Facebook Mural
62   New Directions Publishing
64   iHeartRadio
66   Sony Green
68   Merrill Lynch
70   Dunkin' Donuts
72   National Campaign
      Against Youth Violence
78   New York City 2012
      Olympics Bid
80   United States Holocaust
      Memorial Museum
84   Broadway.com
86   2014 FIFA World Cup Logo
88   H2H Sports
90   Snapple
92   Goodwill Outdoor
      Ad Campaign
94   Royal Shakespeare
      Company
96   Verizon
98   Starwood and Hotels.com
100   Wells Fargo
102   Zipcar
104   Coca-Cola
106   Tree Saver
108   Digicel and Avaya

Developing an icon or a logo for a brand requires a deep understanding of the product or service. The icon should be representative of the company's values and commitment to its customers and be easily recognizable. Some are complicated and some are quite simple and straightforward. Personally, I like simple. But, unfortunately, a lot of the brand decisions get made by committees, so the process can sometimes be grueling—lots of revisions, disagreements about what is and isn't working, and in my case, lots of killed icons that resurface later in other projects.

I like reviving old drawings and turning them into new marks for a completely different concept. It's fun to see where they go sometimes because I don't even see it when I first put pencil to paper.

National Quality Center Logo

Repurposing with a purpose

CLIENT
Sagmeister Inc.

ART DIRECTORS
Stefan Sagmeister
Matthias Ernstberger

The National Quality Center supervises and supports hospitals receiving funding to fight AIDS and work with patients. They control the quality of the care patients receive and distribute educational materials.

I met with Stefan Sagmeister, and we did some sketches. He had drawn some faces in his sketchbook and they were pretty good, so I sort of riffed on that, and then we ended up putting some type on it. After looking at it, I realized it was very gender specific, and I thought they wouldn't be able to use it. I redid it with the ribbon as two people who were supporting one another, not gender specific. The original drawing of the person holding another person was done for *TIME* magazine in the late '90s, and I just sort of repurposed it.

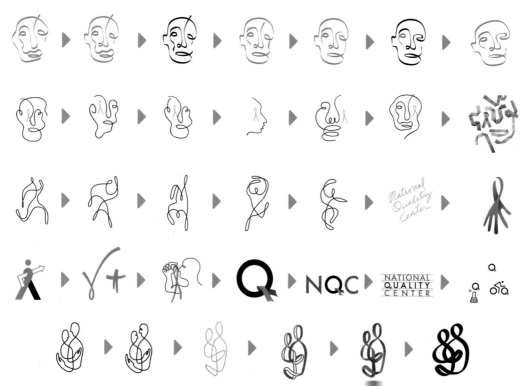

It became clear quickly that creating a symbol that references the AIDS ribbon—by far the most visible and established symbol for the epidemic—would be a viable strategy.

Showing a person helping someone else turned out to be a rather literal translation of the theme—in this case, it worked.

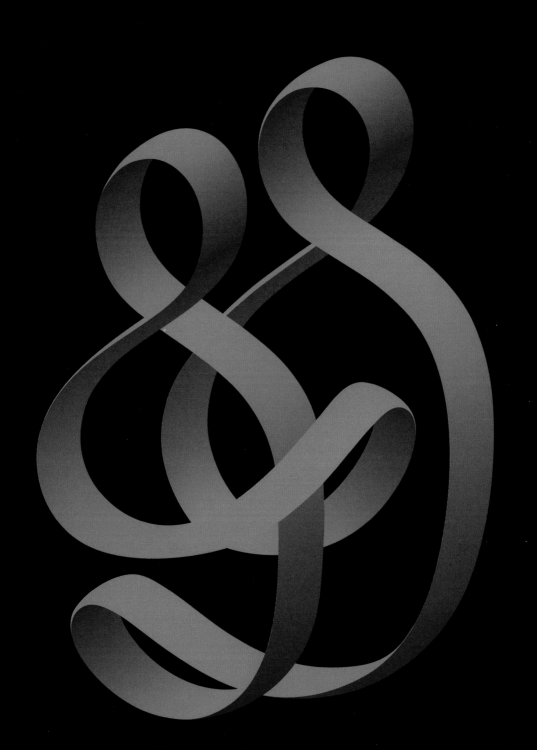

Monopoly Makeover

Updating an iconic gesture

CLIENT
Hasbro

ART DIRECTOR
Jason Taylor

Several years ago, Monopoly called and basically asked me to update the icons on the classic board game. The intent here was to give all of the icons a singular, recognizable voice. The original icons looked like clip art that had been photocopied a hundred times—you couldn't distinguish the lines on the icons any longer. I had to redraw each icon so the lines were crisp and clear.

Some were just cleaned up, while others, like the police officer, were changed altogether. I drew several sketches of the officer, trying to get the arm and hand just right. In the end, I turned it slightly, so his elbow is actually in the corner of the game board, and his arm and hand are larger, pointing players in the right direction. Ultimately, they didn't use anything I gave them, but at least they didn't pay me with Monopoly money.

Original Monopoly Board

Suggested Design Update

1   2   3   4   5   6

When to create an evolution and not a revolution.

The integrity and familiarity of the original cop needed to be maintained to not offend anyone. There was no rhyme or reason for the lines in the original drawing. For instance, the only outlines used in the blue uniform were for the hat and collar, which makes no sense. I basically took the same ingredients of the drawing, but made it consistent.

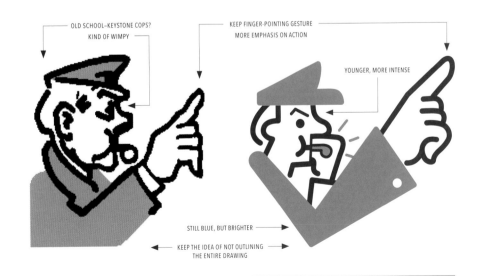

OLD SCHOOL–KEYSTONE COPS?
KIND OF WIMPY

KEEP FINGER-POINTING GESTURE
MORE EMPHASIS ON ACTION

YOUNGER, MORE INTENSE

STILL BLUE, BUT BRIGHTER

KEEP THE IDEA OF NOT OUTLINING
THE ENTIRE DRAWING

Liberty Mutual

Modernizing Lady Liberty

CLIENT
The Sterling Group

CREATIVE DIRECTOR
Debbie Millman

ART DIRECTOR
Kim Berlin

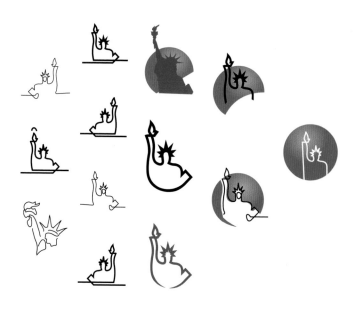

The original logo for this insurance company had an image of the Statue of Liberty, and it was dated and conservative. It also looked terrible when it was reduced or reversed. They still wanted a statue with a face, which just complicated it. I didn't think it would work, but I let it all play out, incorporating a lot of different elements and lots of workups and revisions. I tried to warm it up a bit, too, because the current logo was cold and rigid. It's a big ask for a simple icon.

Inspiration
I borrowed some elements from this for global reference in the logo concepts.

Some of these were too fussy; others were too simple. The extra lines weren't helping the idea.

One way to skin this cat would be to lose the torch within the firelight. I kept reducing it and lost all the extra lines. The last one works the best. I also liked the idea of putting it in a shield, but the client didn't.

Shield

I liked the idea of putting this in a shield because it represents protection or guard against accidents. But the shield doesn't need to have Lady Liberty in it. It doesn't really feel that strong.

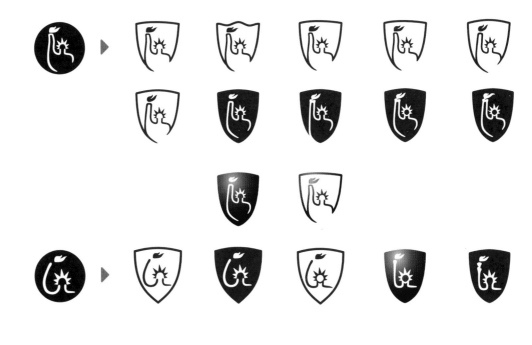

I've never been a big fan of transparent marks because they don't reproduce on napkins, embossed in plastic, etc., but this fluid mark isn't bad. If we trash the globe, there may be room to grow this one.

Before we started
the first iteration,
we all agreed
that Lady Liberty
wasn't going to
change from their
existing vector
design.

REFINED FORMS

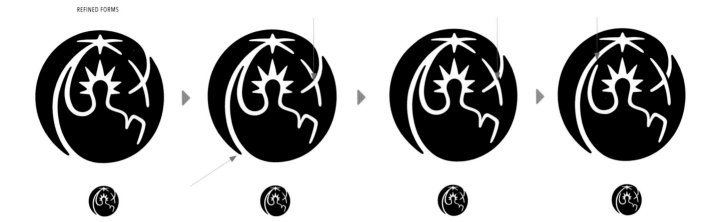

Zynga

It's a dog-eat-dog world in 19 pixels

CLIENT
Odopod

ART DIRECTOR
Guthrie Dolan

One of the hurdles of designing icons for this size is how to get something down to its bare essence in 19 pixels. It's not easy. Then there's the branding challenge—what to keep, what to toss out, and what goes where.

My first thought was to grab some old drawings of dogs for reference. Then, I went about retrofitting the mutt into a square.

I tried making sequential gestures in hopes of tailoring messages, lassoing the bulldog into a colorful, universal mass. Nothing seemed to work. We tried a circus tent, a trophy, puzzles, and different gaming devices. What remained true, and not worth the change, was that the owner's dog, named Zynga, was not going anywhere.

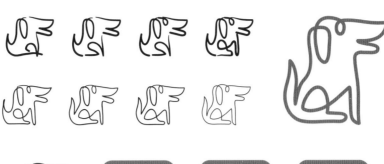

The dog can sit, lie down, beg, pant, bark, whatever. He's a link, or connection, to your (best) gamer friends.

ALTERNATE MORE PLAYFUL LOOK

Should it play a faster, more functional role? Maybe it links side to side with other icons that carry Zynga's characteristics.

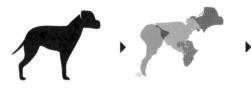 

Zynga unites the world through games.

I tried turning the dog's leash into a mouse and illustrating the shapes of the continents on the dog in relation to connecting the world through games. Ultimately, they didn't work because they're too detailed to be small.

This is inspired by the Joker character. It's a carnival/festival joker-esque type that broke into a singular symbol.

We tried the dog in various poses in conjunction with a trophy. The trophy could also substitute as a symbol for the *Y* when used in a word mark.

I think this one has a sporty/mythic/memorable quality. We've seen all kinds of winged beasts, but never an American bulldog.

This was an idea that didn't catch fire.

We tried various applications of a cityscape of San Francisco, but this idea was too detailed.

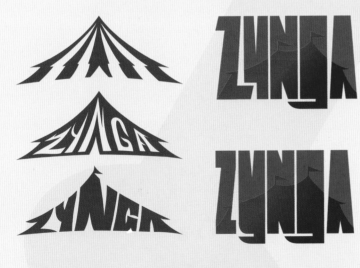

We also tried various puzzle ideas, integrating different interpretations of people and the world and applying a tint.

Yogurt Company

This was a classic barnyard tragedy

CLIENT
Pentagram

ART DIRECTORS
Michael Bierut
Joe Marianek

My first round included full-bodied sheep and cows.

The sheep is starting to look evil.

DECENT, BUT TOO MUCH WOOL

LET'S MAKE IT GEOMETRIC

I'm not feeling the circle, but they requested it.

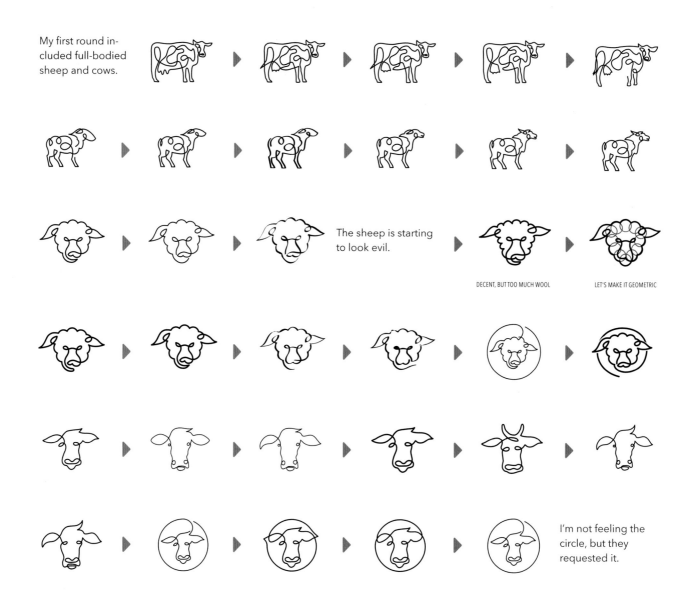

Pentagram was hired to redesign the brand for a highly visible yogurt company. They contracted me to rework some of the icons on the packaging. I went back and forth with Joe Marianek, the art director at Pentagram working on the project. He would make small tweaks/suggestions, to which I'd respond with my own.

As Joe recalls, "The yogurt project was a classic barnyard tragedy. I remember that you made some cows, then some sheep, a few goats, and eventually a mule. By that point, we had finally worn the client out and they decided to stick with their existing wordmark in the 1995 hit font Broadband."

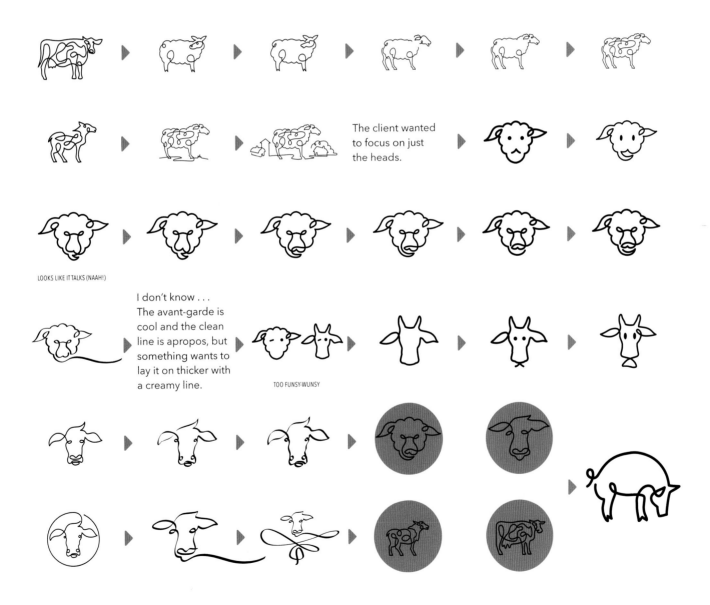

The client wanted to focus on just the heads.

LOOKS LIKE IT TALKS (NAAH!)

I don't know . . . The avant-garde is cool and the clean line is apropos, but something wants to lay it on thicker with a creamy line.

TOO FUNSY-WUNSY

Apple

Exploring a connected world

CLIENT
Apple

ART DIRECTOR
Joe Marianek

Provenance and reuse are interesting themes in my work. On deadline, I often find myself building things from scrap and then redrawing them painstakingly and frustratingly to no avail. Big clients and important applications carry nondisclosure paperwork, and you have to be mindful about process and ownership. I often find myself doodling sketches and ideas in the margins that are never shown to anyone until I can find the file and glean some knowledge or nugget. Sadly, going down the rabbit hole often finds a beautiful mess that chaos claims. Nonetheless, being stubborn and persistent allows me to consistently cheat redrawing work, picking off meat from a fresh kill.

Facebook Mural

Melding images and information into a unified language

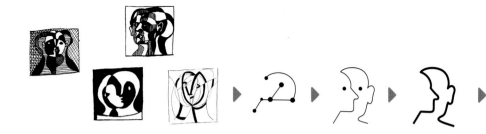

CLIENT
Facebook

ART DIRECTORS
Ben Barry
Josh Higgins
Scott Boms

Right:
The animals on the right
are Picasso tracings that
inspired some of the
mural method.

My work for Facebook has been years
in the making. Initially, in 2008, they
wanted me to do a T-shirt design, but
it didn't work out. A year or so later,
Facebook designer Ben Barry hired
me to design icons for the log-out
page, but this page also facilitated log-
ins, so I just called it the front page. We
spent months going back and forth,
improving certain aspects of the page,

Above:
These Picasso images were used as
reference for the progression of the
faces. Depending on your point of view,
these faces mean "communication" or
"sharing" or "humanity." But it's also a
trick or visual illusion that draws you
into the conversation.

and for the most part, had a good time.
Months rolled by waiting for approv-
als, and after a year, I was told that the
project wasn't going to happen.

Fast-forward seven years, and the
new art director, Josh Higgins, along
with Scott Boms, called and asked if
they could use my design as a kind
of wallpaper in the central lobby of
the new headquarters in Palo Alto,
California. The connection motif, spun
together with larger profiles and tiny
linear icons, was well received and later adopted in other Facebook offices,
most recently Los Angeles.

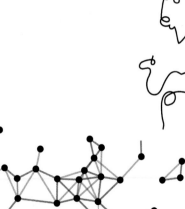

FACEBOOK LOG IN/ OUT PAGE, 2009-10

FACEBOOK LOG IN/OUT COMPED INTO FRANK GEHRY'S HQ, PALO ALTO

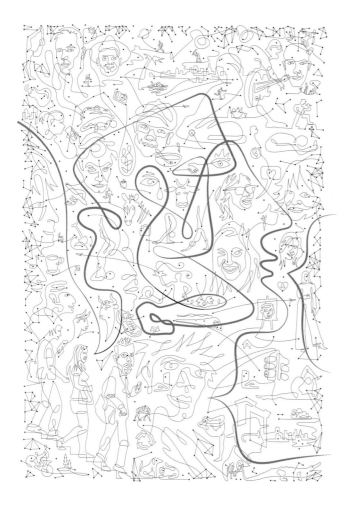

I tried to slip lots of icons into it with the intent that someone would see it and get the idea that you could use these icons in other applications. I put all kinds of macro and micro images into the mural. Facebook is all about interactions between people, so there are lots of faces (many are friends) and animals and activities. All the things people brag about on Facebook are there—their travels, their accomplishments, their kids, their pets, etc. It all ties into the community at large.

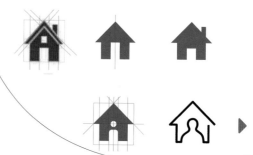

All these disparate ideas and gestures create a new iconic language that can be shared and understood universally. Going poop? There's an icon for that. Going sailing? There's an icon for that. Get it?

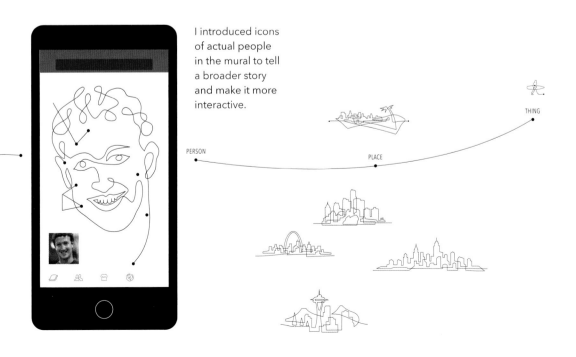

I introduced icons of actual people in the mural to tell a broader story and make it more interactive.

PERSON PLACE THING

I created a series of simple gestures that could be used as a whole new way to communicate on Facebook. These are connections that express ideas about life, love, loss, and so on.

This is just a simple exploration as to how these gestures can be used in your Facebook feed.

Like

Love

HaHa

Wow

Sad

Mad

Ohh...

Hey, look, it's Sampah! And Jeff is bragging about his running pace again. And Laura had a baby girl.

Micro to macro. Like to love. There is always a way to make old ideas new again by looking at it, tweaking it, and distilling the elements to their simplest gesture. The journey to finding the timeless solution can takes years—sometimes decades.

New Directions Publishing

The project that almost killed me

CLIENT
New Directions Publishing

ART DIRECTOR
Rodrigo Corral

This appears to be a standard run-through of turning an image into a one-line assemblage. Trust me, it wasn't. At the time, when art director Rodrigo Corral called, I neglected to tell him that I was battling what I thought was food poisoning. More on that later. I felt terrible, but I was able to sit at the computer and read the brief, start drawing new parts, and form a strategy.

I did some research on New Directions and found that the original logo was designed by Heinz Henghes. I didn't understand the logo's meaning in regard to New Directions, but it's been around for seventy-five years, unchanged. As I went about researching Henghes's work, I discovered he was quite an artist. In fact, he was a sculptor, and the inspiration for the logo came from a drawing of one of his sculptures.

But, before I could do anything, I had to lie on the floor on my stomach because my abdomen was throbbing in pain. I was unable to eat or drink for eight days, all the while hallucinating from the intense pain, until I finally drove myself to the hospital (after losing 27 pounds [12 kg]). But, not before I turned in some sketches to Rodrigo.

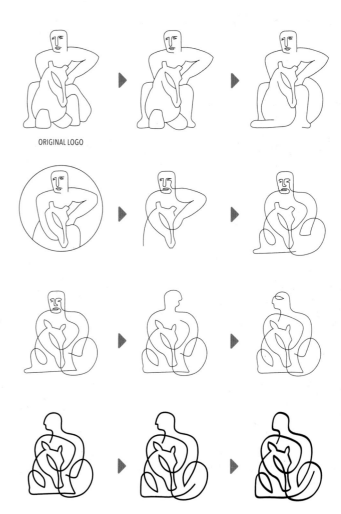

ORIGINAL LOGO

As it turned out, my appendix had burst. The doctor thought I was crazy. He said, "What the hell were you thinking? You almost died!" What can I say? I'm a slave to my craft.

When I got out of the hospital, after two botched surgeries, I drew a visual sequence to make sense of how the logo could work. Believe it or not, it worked. We sold the damn thing. Happy 75th anniversary, New Directions.

If you squint your eyes you can see a man petting a horse. That's all I know. I was hallucinating for Chrissake.

iHeartRadio

Taking a literal approach

CLIENT
iHeartMedia

ART DIRECTOR
Josh Klenart

A heart. A radio. A connection between the organic vibrations of each individual sentient being and an Internet radio platform?

Easy.

Milton Glaser nailed it in 1977, with that buxom red valentine, so why not start there? Fun fact! Did you know the heart pictogram has tons of conflicting origin stories? As in, maybe it's supposed to be ivy leaves, representing fidelity. Or it could be a pair of breasts or buttocks. Or I (heart) the story about it being a picture of an ancient Roman contraceptive plant called silphium.

After presenting several iterations with the heart, a person, and a radio, there was sort of a debate about how pure the icons could look. I thought they should be a single line, but someone at the company wanted to go with two lines on some of them. Then they went through weeks of testing to make sure they were readable at certain sizes. They've done a pretty good job of implementing the icons. I see them on billboards around New York.

Help! He wants me
to meet his parents!

Help! She says it's more
than a three-night stand!

Am I air-quoting myself?

This one felt like a simple design, yet
with enough depth to draw out the
different meanings.

Music News & Talk Sports What's On

Location Hosts & DJs Subscription Auto Play

Favorites Video Recent Stations Trash

Sony Green

An attempt at going green goes nowhere

CLIENT
Sony

ART DIRECTOR
Kyle Amdahl

When a company decides to become eco-friendly, you see all the usual visual clichés: earth, recycling logo, trees, images of nature, etc., all in green. The most important component is often left out: humans.

Where eyes enter an icon is as important as where they exit. You should rewind the process and think of the movement as meaning and song. Scientists have suggested that keeping images broad in nature and form allows for more meaning and creativity. If you put too much emphasis—as is the case here—on the leaves, then you only remember the leaves and not the recycling and the head (humanity) in the order. You're trying to capture the feeling as well as the process. It's not easy.

Over the course of this exploratory, we presented various ways to enter and leave the image, but could never quite nail down something that worked for digital recycling.

Original Client Sketch
The original client sketch was based on a sketch of mine that they had seen.

LAME!

NOT TERRIBLE

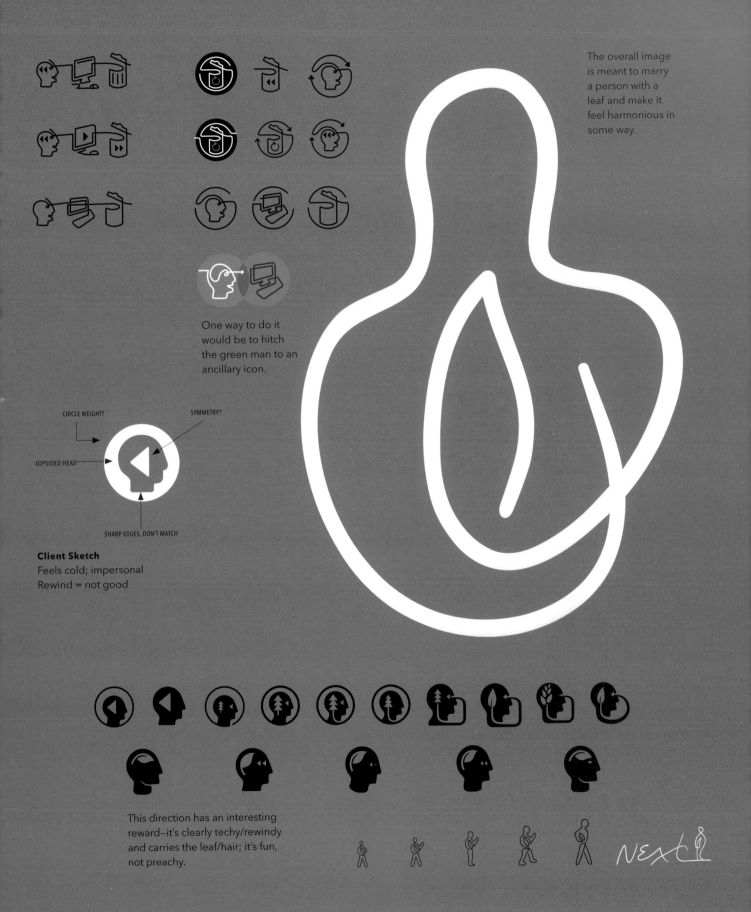

The overall image is meant to marry a person with a leaf and make it feel harmonious in some way.

One way to do it would be to hitch the green man to an ancillary icon.

CIRCLE WEIGHT?

SYMMETRY?

LOPSIDED HEAD

SHARP EDGES, DON'T MATCH

Client Sketch
Feels cold; impersonal
Rewind = not good

This direction has an interesting reward—it's clearly techy/rewindy and carries the leaf/hair; it's fun, not preachy.

Next

Merrill Lynch

Taking the BS out of the bull

CLIENT
Time Inc.

ART DIRECTOR
Cindy Becker

Okay, so the assignment wasn't to re-design the logo. I threw that in for fun. I castrated the bull and made it linear—you know, tamed him a bit. They didn't buy it, but I wasn't expecting them to.

The real deal was drawing the icons for an app that in-house employees would use. You'll see a lot of similar things at play here that I've done before. I did a flat graphic, similar to what Microsoft did, and put things into squares. This is an instrument I've played many, many times.

Fun Facts about Bulls!

❶ Bulls cannot see the color red. They actually charge at matadors' capes because they can't stand that annoying flappy sound the capes make.

❶ In Hinduism, there is a holy bull named Nandi who is Shiva's sidekick.

❶ On Wall Street, the bull statue was originally named Mindy McCuddles, Bovine Extraordinaire.

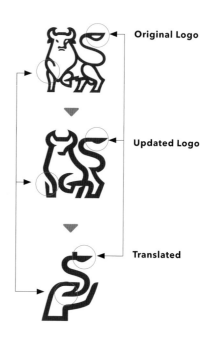

Original Logo

Updated Logo

Translated

Final Complete Icon Set

FINANCE

HEALTH

FAMILY

HOME

WORK

GIVING

LEISURE

BLOG

CHECK LIST

Q&A

SLIDE SHOW

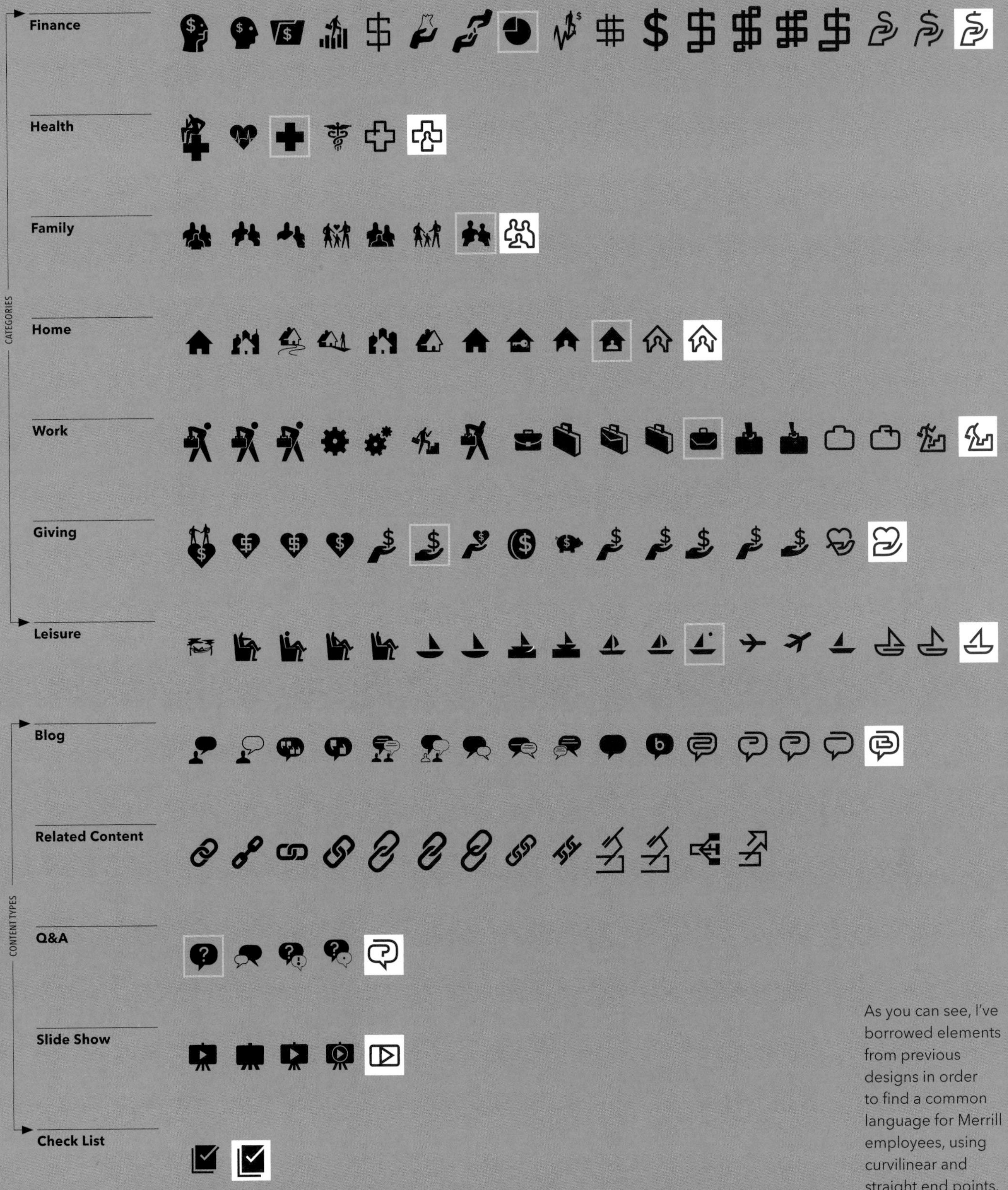

CATEGORIES

Finance

Health

Family

Home

Work

Giving

Leisure

CONTENT TYPES

Blog

Related Content

Q&A

Slide Show

Check List

As you can see, I've borrowed elements from previous designs in order to find a common language for Merrill employees, using curvilinear and straight end points.

Dunkin' Donuts

Considering the potential of an existing mark

CLIENT
Self-initiated

In 1998, the heads of Dunkin' Donuts decided to rebrand themselves with a whimsical Styrofoam cup icon to remind patrons that they serve coffee as well as donuts. This somewhat rustic icon is totally out of character with the diner aesthetic inherent in the brand's typography. Did anyone notice? Maybe. Maybe not. I guess it depends on where you sit. I certainly did. Let's stop and take a look at how the rebranding could have taken the higher road. Shall we?

Above:
The 1998 rebranded Dunkin' Donuts logo.

Right:
The aforementioned promise (see cup A) is seen nowhere on Dunkin's website. The Styrofoam cup B is noted in the advertising, while the paper cup C is on the website. The lack of continuity is not surprising.

   You could surmise that the brand managers of Dunkin' Donuts claim this disoriented promise is a realization that, in relation to competitor Starbucks, the design is an accurate representation of the Dunkin' experience: Cheap(er), "no nonsense" coffee accessible to anyone, anywhere, anytime. You could say it feels more "fast food nation" than the "comfortable diner" you enjoyed years ago. Am I right?

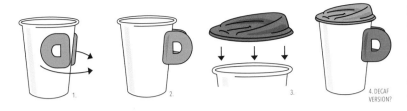

Left:
In my "what if" scenario, we start with personalizing the experience. The competitor uses those brown, ridged cozies that slip over the cup, keeping your fingers from the heat. Styrofoam accomplishes the same feat, but at a cost to both the supplier (it is 25 percent more expensive than paper) as well as the consumer (once poured, Styrofoam dilutes the taste of coffee). Styrofoam also puts more of a strain on the environment—it isn't recyclable. The smart, no-frills idea (above) immediately engages the consumer with the product. As you pull back the flaps, it becomes your Dunkin' coffee creation. Not printing on the cup saves the company even more money. It's a win, win, win.

GIFT CARDS

T-SHIRTS AND HOODIES

One other thing I noticed as I did my research on Dunkin' was the lack of imagination displayed within its promotional product line. The logo is simply slapped onto merchandise with no care whatsoever. And why? The Dunkin' logo stands as one of the best of all time! It should be celebrated. The idea that people still dunk their donuts is obviously passé, but the logo is a timeless hallmark of American diner culture.

Kids love donuts. You know it. I know it. Kids know it. Why not have some fun with it? Sure, they aren't healthy, but products produced with an activity (i.e., roller-skating) safeguard you against health critics who will cry foul. For the rest of us, we can choose to accessorize with simple items that extend the brand seamlessly. Who knew coffee and donuts were good advertising icons?

Above:
This is what putting the logo into action would look like. By inserting creativity and function within the logotype, you breathe life into an otherwise docile mark. The beauty of the ideas contained within this exploratory is that they extend meaning and whimsy to a sleeping giant.

Left:
Okay. I've gone and done it now—I've messed up the logo. But, what if, say, you had a coffee stand in Times Square? Donuts? Hmm. Not so much. People want a coffee, bagel, donut, or croissant, and that's it. They're outta there. It may not work in all areas, but it's a viable extension if needs change.

Below: Brand evolution.

National Campaign Against Youth Violence

Using clip art for inspiration

CLIENT
FCB/Templin Brink

ART DIRECTORS
Joel Templin
Erik T. Johnson

CO-ILLUSTRATOR
Erik T. Johnson

Late in Bill Clinton's presidency, he formed an initiative called the National Campaign Against Youth Violence, following the Columbine shootings. Whatever we came up with, it needed to symbolize hope, peace, and America. I was sifting through an old clip art book, and I saw a bird that was interesting. Erik Johnson—with whom I was collaborating—and I went back and forth and beat it up. We cut and pasted and photocopied it a bunch of times. It morphed from using hands as wings to incorporating the bird into the palm of the hand. Everybody loved it, so we also produced some posters.

Is a bird in a hand worth two in the bush? Ironically, this initiative was dropped during the George "Dubya" Bush presidency.

Thinking on Paper

"Drawing is essential to understanding form."

–Milton Glaser

There's no better way to think in design than with a pencil and paper. It's more natural. And you have a more tactile relationship with your hand and brain. The computer limits your ability to change gears and have free-flowing thoughts. Milton Glaser said it best: "Drawing is essential to understanding form. . . . The act of drawing makes me conscious of what I'm looking at. If I wasn't drawing, I sense that I wouldn't be seeing."

apple

Stella

Globe

world

Flags

Lots of t
Within
Apple

electronic
jewelry
Auto
Sporting
home deco
kitchen

anime

New York City 2012 Olympics Bid

Don't hate the Games, hate the players

CLIENT
COLLINS

ART DIRECTORS
Brian Collins
Brian Darling

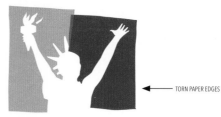

TORN PAPER EDGES

Left:
Experiments
in shape
and overlaps.

This project is something lettering artist Jessica Hische might call "procrastiworking." The icons to the right were designed half-heartedly in my "free" time with an accompanying logo "I Olympics NY." I tossed it on my website a year or so before bid logos began popping up. Once that started happening, my old cohort Brian Collins from BIG called and ask if I could illustrate an idea one of his designers (Brian Darling) had come up with using the Statue of Liberty for inspiration.

Lady Liberty spent the last century or so taking in the tired, the poor, the huddled masses yearning to get a hot pretzel and some fake Chanel bags on Canal Street, only to get stopped and frisked in front of the Staten Island Ferry?

This is wrong with a capital ONG. I did a sketch of the Lady while she was getting felt up and questioned—the only thing they could accuse her of was aggressive oxidation. I thought surely my image would wake the world up from its self-induced coma of narcissism.

In the end, London came calling and we lost the bid.

Above:
NYC graffiti with spray paint.

Below:
Expandable mark to include Olympic rings and NYC2012.

NYC2012

NYC2012

Above:
A play on Milton Glaser's famous I (heart) NY logo.

Right:
Icons for Olympic events and other NYC activities.

United States Holocaust Memorial Museum

Competing in the big leagues for a highly charged identity system—and losing

CLIENT
United States Holocaust
Memorial Museum

COLLABORATORS
Stefan Sagmeister
Thomas Fuchs

I was contacted by a consultant to pitch a new identity for the Holocaust Museum, along with nine other designers. Before stepping into the ring, though, I had to prove that I had billed more than $50,000 for a similar project—which, of course, I hadn't—so I teamed up with Stefan Sagmeister. We were competing against Paula Scher at Pentagram, so we were pretty certain we weren't going to get the job, but it was intriguing nonetheless.

I actually became kind of obsessed with this one. I met Thomas Fuchs at a bar one night and we sketched out ideas on an envelope. I ended up taking some of those concepts and exploring them further. It was a tricky dance: on one hand, this had to be impactful and provocative, but on the other, it also couldn't play into the old emotions associated with the Holocaust. The museum wanted to attract younger patrons and inform them of the realities

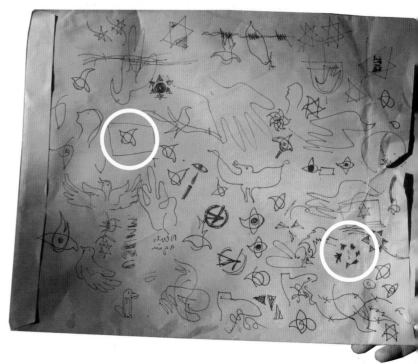

Based on the sketches I did at the bar, I focused in on these two concepts.

The initial thinking behind transforming the Star of David arose from the idea of a Holocaust candle and remembrance. This morphed into utilizing the shapes of the flame, the eye, and the dove with a one, two, three punch.

UNITED STATES

HOLOCAUST

MEMORIAL

MUSEUM

WASHINGTON DC

Initially in the top sketch, I had the bird holding an olive branch, but then decided to remove it. In the end, this entire idea didn't make sense conceptually.

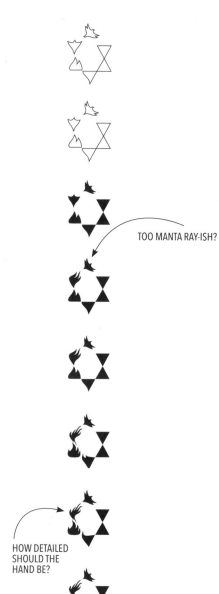

TOO MANTA RAY-ISH?

HOW DETAILED
SHOULD THE
HAND BE?

**MORE ABSTRACT
OR LITERAL BIRD?**

THE CONCEPTUAL STORY

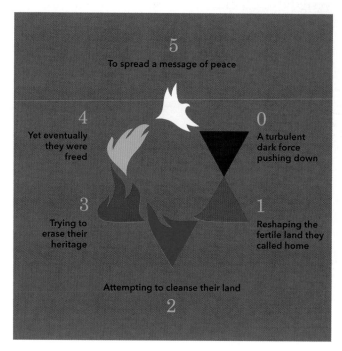

5
To spread a message of peace

4
Yet eventually
they were
freed

0
A turbulent
dark force
pushing down

3
Trying to
erase their
heritage

1
Reshaping the
fertile land they
called home

Attempting to cleanse their land
2

of genocide in present time happening around the world.

So in my explorations, an eye sort of emerged over a line drawing of a flame, and inside the eye, I drew a dove. I liked it, but thought it might be too literal and emotional. So, I scrapped that and switched my focus to the Star of David. Using the star's six points/triangles, I

translated different ideas—land, water, flame, hand, and a dove—to encapsulate the full narrative.

But, just as I had predicted, we lost the bid to Paula. It was nice to lose to her. I have a lot of respect for who she is and what she does.

ANIMATION POTENTIAL

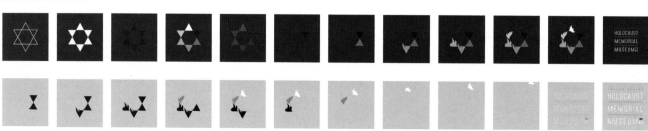

For the final workup, I decided to scrap the colors and change direction with custom typography by Robert Festino.

HOLOCAUST

MEMORIAL

MUSEUM DC

Broadway.com

Because if I don't see *Hamilton*, my life will mean nothing

CLIENT
Serino Coyne

ART DIRECTORS
Vinny Sainato
Jay Cooper
Michelle Willems

Broadway! The dazzle, the razzle, the neon marquees so bright they eat up the sky.

$100 a seat
+ $150 for the sitter
+ $85 for some fried calamari and two Pinot Grigios
+ $5.75 if we take the subway or $35 if the N/R stops and we have to Uber
+ $10 for a bag of crinkly mints to take out during the overture
+ $10,000 for another year of therapy to deal with (spoiler alert) the abandonment issues that are evoked in the penultimate scene
———————————————
= A night to remember!

BROADWAY.com

Broadway.com is the known entity, but Key Brand Entertainment also owns several other large entities, and the design problem was bringing them all together under one umbrella.

WEBSITE NAVIGATION

I tried to distill the wording and the elements into a common theme by using typography to adjoin the key term with a more expressive term. The icons are trying to illustrate the literal interpretations for each group.

BROADWAY.com

BROADWAY across AMERICA

KEY BRAND Entertainment

BROADWAYBOX.com

GROUP SALES Box Office

BROADWAY Channel

Yellow too light?

Why, thank you, it's pashmina, of course.

If you can find the missing finger, you get a prize.

I have a three top by the jukebox that's still waiting for its flapjacks.

Repurposed Weight Watchers icon.

Mezzanine going Zax and Balcony going Zax.

There are no small parts, only small stages.

★ BROADWAY.com

★ BROADWAY across AMERICA

★ KEY BRAND Entertainment

★ BROADWAYBOX.com

★ GROUP SALES Box Office

★ BROADWAY Channel

2014 FIFA World Cup Logo

Brazil's 2014 Logotastrophy

CLIENT
Self-initiated

I'm a huge soccer fan, so I was really excited about going to the World Cup in Brazil in 2014—until I saw this logo. There are so many things wrong with it.

No offense to all the soccer stars of the world who happen to be frogs. You deserve representation, too. But this looks like an amphibious attack on the 2014, and the color gradients are all wrong.

I started my redesign by giving the froggy fingers some slimming gloves. Keepers wear gloves. No glove, no logo love!

There's also no need to make the ® and © characters so big. It's overpowering.

I redrew the hands, disconnecting the fingers from each other. I also removed the year, which not only simplified the logo, but also simplified the color palette. This logo needs to be able to work in black and white, as well, which the old one didn't. The type was also clunky and cartoonish. I simplified the main copy with a simple sans serif and did a hand-written Brazil to give it some swagger.

REGISTERED AND COPYRIGHT SYMBOLS ARE OUT OF PROPORTION.

FINGERS ARE POORLY DEFINED.

THE PROPORTIONS OF THE TROPHY ARE NOT CORRECTLY DRAWN.

Above:
The proportions of the trophy are not correctly drawn.

Above:
Most important, the logo needs to be reproduced in many different methods—embroidery, silk screen, printing on Coke cans—which means it needs to be easily converted into black and white without losing its core structure.

Above:
Redrawn using the traditional Brazilian flag colors with distinctive fingers in gloves. A looser script echoes the flow of the Brazilian game.

Below:
Another thing people like to know when you're designing their identity is how it works across several touch points. I would have liked to see an application that utilized more of the colors and elements from the flag. Repetition builds strength.

H2H Sports

The iN DEMAND sports channel that was never in demand

CLIENT
iN DEMAND

COLLABORATOR
Thomas Fuchs

You win some. You lose some.

You lose some more. You talk about that time you were winning because that was really fun, right?

And then you lose some more. That's the story here.

The client asked for a logo for its new sports channel called Head2Head. I went back to the studio—where I was working with Thomas Fuchs, at the time—and started doing research. Turns out, "H2H" was already owned by another company. I told the client, but they didn't seem to care.

Oh well. Fuchs and I went back and forth with some of these sketches. We'd write down words, go through sketchbooks, and arbitrarily work with the letters and number. Things that are television-related tend to be in a circle—think CBS, ABC, etc. It automatically has a television feel if it's circular, so I focused on that.

But you already know. It didn't happen—the channel or the logo. We lose again.

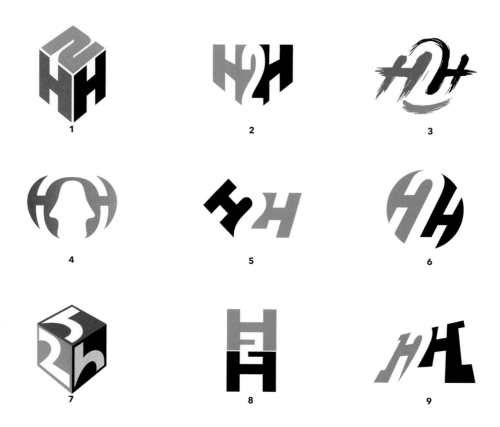

I felt this one was
the most distilled
of the variations we
explored. The use
of the circle seemed
to make sense for a
television channel.

Snapple

Embracing the warmth of the sun

CLIENT
Cliff Freeman & Partners

CREATIVE DIRECTOR
Tom Christman

ACCOUNT DIRECTOR
Jeff McClelland

CO-ILLUSTRATOR
Christoph Niemann

Whenever you think of Coke, certain symbols or images come to mind, such as the ribbon or the bottle. When it came to Snapple, I wanted them to own the shape of their iconic bottle—something that made a nice popping sound when opened. They'd never thought to wrap their arms around that shape, which was significant in the minds of consumers.

Once I redrew the iconic sun symbol, I went about laying it into various applications and poses, trying to get a handle on its flexibility (or adaptability). Then, I gave Christoph Niemann a call to do another version. His was friendlier and could animate in fun ways. Unfortunately, none of our work seemed to gain any traction, but we had a decent time working together.

I tried various uses of the sun and integrated the bottle shape with the type.

I sent my version over to Christoph for an additional translation of the sun that could be animated. His version seemed friendlier than mine.

Goodwill Outdoor Ad Campaign

Skip the toll roads

CLIENT
Agency in Kansas

COLLABORATORS
Thomas Fuchs
James Victore

Many of the assignments I translate are from smaller agencies in the Midwest region, where service to the client is paramount. In this case, the agency sent over some comps of the chosen campaign. I asked the art director what style would be appropriate and did we really need to have a license plate with condensed Helvetica (which isn't the face that plates use). The copy was quite good. The problem, as I saw it, was engaging people with a memorable, quick statement. These were outdoor boards, so the messaging had to be instant. People don't have time to read the entire headline driving 75 mph.

My initial thinking was met with screeching tires. I recall having a conversation with the art director about the use of the logo (designed in 1972 by Joe Salame) and whether we could use it. They said no. Why? No reason. Just make it work according to the comps. The problem was

There is so much equity tied to the trademark. And after some research, I found that it is still in use, though not every branch opts to use it in their materials. In my mind, this dilutes the brand. Goodwill should have the same message in Arizona as it does in Maine.

Left:
Initial sketch from James Victore.

Agency Comps

Direction One
Agency comps (at left) conveyed style not in an illustrator's vocabulary. The initial idea was to reinterpret each headline into an iconic graphic that married the messaging.

I didn't get the comps, a fact that I should've stressed more adamantly from the outset. I sucked it up and tried another "friendly linear" style that also hit a brick wall. I was torn. Should I keep heading down this road? Am I serving Goodwill's cause or just carrying forth the agency's wishes? After commiserating with a few friends, Thomas Fuchs and James Victore (James doodled the key, which I finished out, and Thomas designed the smiley car, above), I decided the best thing to do would be to simply stand my ground. I gave them three ideas: here's what you asked for, here's what could be done in the middle, and here's what I'm suggesting, which is drastically different. What do you think happened?

Direction Two
Here's another more literal attempt to try and appease the agency.

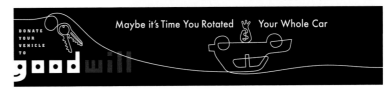

Royal Shakespeare Company

Taking liberties with theatrical references

CLIENT
Royal Shakespeare
Company

ART DIRECTOR
Andy Williams

The Royal Shakespeare Company hired me to do a series of spot illustrations for an online newsletter for their educational unit. The themes I was given for the spots were develop, share, and transform. While working on those, I started toying with the RSC logo. It doesn't have any proprietary emphasis, and it sure isn't in keeping with Shakespeare. I mean, Futura?

I was playing with the letter shapes, and the "S" started looking like a face. I liked the theatrical quality of that, so I kept at it. I also used Trajan for the copy beneath the logo. There's a running joke that Trajan is the go-to font in the movie title industry, so why not use it for a theater logo?

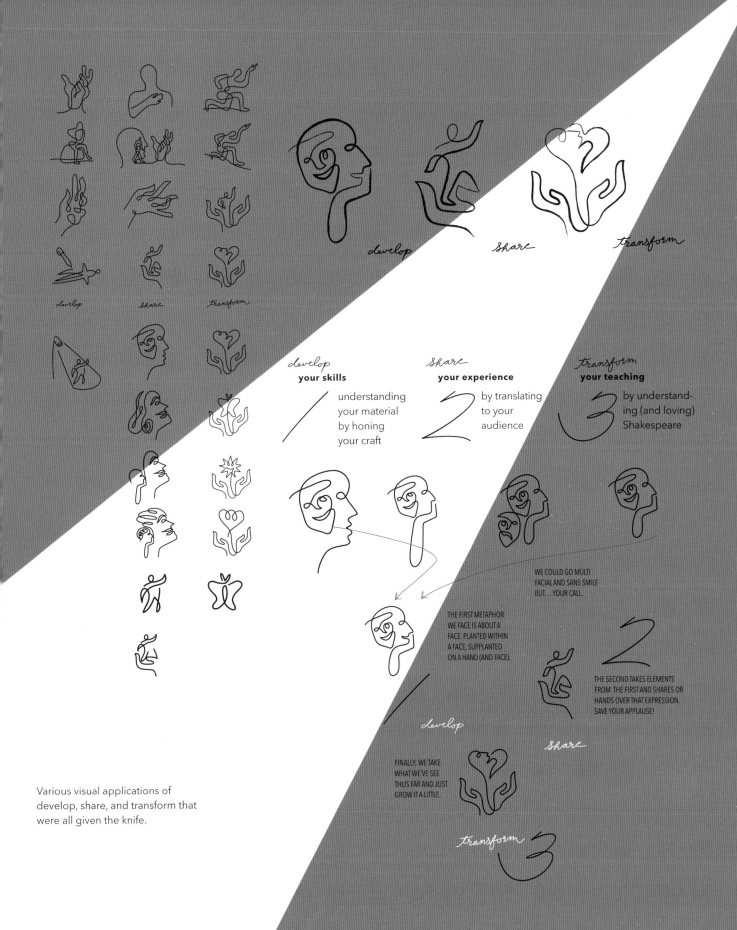

develop
your skills

1 understanding
your material
by honing
your craft

share
your experience

2 by translating
to your
audience

transform
your teaching

3 by understand-
ing (and loving)
Shakespeare

WE COULD GO MULTI
FACIAL AND SANS SMILE
BUT. . . YOUR CALL.

THE FIRST METAPHOR
WE FACE IS ABOUT A
FACE. PLANTED WITHIN
A FACE, SUPPLANTED
ON A HAND (AND FACE).

THE SECOND TAKES ELEMENTS
FROM THE FIRST AND SHARES OR
HANDS OVER THAT EXPRESSION.
SAVE YOUR APPLAUSE!

develop

share

FINALLY, WE TAKE
WHAT WE'VE SEE
THUS FAR AND JUST
GROW IT A LITTLE.

transform 3

Various visual applications of
develop, share, and transform that
were all given the knife.

Verizon

The check mark that keeps on giving

CLIENT
Verizon

AGENCY
Pentagram

ART DIRECTORS
Michael Bierut
Aron Fay
Abby Matousek

In 2015, Pentagram redesigned the Verizon logo, under the direction of Michael Bierut. It's a huge improvement over the previous logo design. As Armin Vit wrote in his critique of the new logo for *Brand New*, "The old logo was truly a bad one. Its main italic wordmark would have survived on its own but the addition of the giant check mark with gradient and the zooming *z* with gradient turned it into a parody of what a corporate logo could be." I couldn't agree more. If you were a surgeon trying to work with that logo, it would be inoperable.

So, when Michael proposed a set of icons to work with the new check mark, I gladly worked 'em up and sent them over. They're not too whimsical or illustrative, but they are distinguishable. There are so many opportunities to expand on the mark and communicate to different audiences, but why would Verizon want to do that? They passed.

Above: Verizon's old logo was widely criticized for years. Their new one—designed by Pentagram—incorporates the red checkmark to the right of the word.

Below: These icons were developed to work with the new check mark and reiterate a singular line method with a typographic feel.

	EXPLORATORY	GENERIC	BRANDED
PHONE			
DESKTOP COMPUTER			
VERIZON U.S. COVERAGE MAP			
WATCH			
SPEEDOMETER			
DOLLAR SYMBOL			
WIRELESS SYMBOL			
ARROW			
HOUSE			

The exploratory for these categories became clear when I drew the desktop computer and began applying the branded Verizon check into the designs. However, the work appeared hokey and forced.

This is a mock-up demonstrating how the icons can communicate the idea of Internet, data, and phone all in one place.

Starwood and Hotels.com

The job that saved BIG

CLIENT
Starwood Hotels & Resorts

DESIGNERS
Erik Johnson
Thomas Vasquez

When I was part of the Brand Integration Group (BIG) at Ogilvy, we were doing the design for the preferred guest rewards for Starwood Hotels. It was one of our first big assignments. Over the course of six months, while our two creative directors were plying away on angles that didn't pan out, this seemingly unimportant job netted close to $2 million and saved us from the chopping block—seriously, if this job had failed, we all would have been fired. We finished the job, a lot

of which was extra (not asked for), such as logos and icons for their master brand, and a year later, they fired Ogilvy and hired another agency to revamp our work.

None of this work was ever used, but I ended up using lots of this stuff—these gestures—later on for Hotels.com and various other things.

That little sun with the key was really good. I remember when I was working on this, Louise Fili came into the office, and she was drawn to the sun design.

Wells Fargo

It's all in the wheels

CLIENT
Wells Fargo

ART DIRECTOR
Alex Dejanosi

Good companies frequently spend time and resources exploring "what if" options. When heritage is considered, designs should reflect a host of deliverables. The stagecoach will always be part of the Wells Fargo logo, but I played with variations of it to make it more accessible. We talked about how the style and craftsmanship play into their heritage and narrative.

None of this was part of the deliverable. They asked me to do a linear version of their logo, and I went in an opposite direction. However, I did supply them with another round of options to meet their needs. As I recall, there were about five illustrators commissioned to reinterpret this logo.

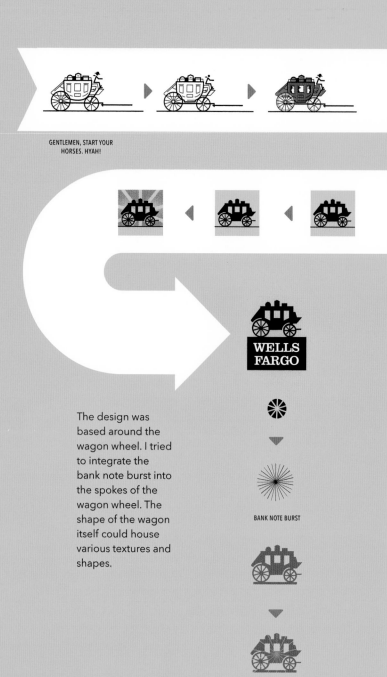

GENTLEMEN, START YOUR HORSES. HYAH!

The design was based around the wagon wheel. I tried to integrate the bank note burst into the spokes of the wagon wheel. The shape of the wagon itself could house various textures and shapes.

WELLS FARGO

BANK NOTE BURST

INCORPORATE INTO THE MARK

JUST HORSES

  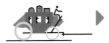   

IT'S NOT ABOUT THE
COWBOYS . . .

It Starts with the Wheel
I'm steering toward using
the wheel and the shape to
carry through.

LESS ⟶ MORE

Logos that are locked
in horizontally are
self-limiting.

HORSES + DRIVER

HORSES + DRIVER + PASSENGERS

HORSES + DRIVER + PASSENGERS + HIGHLIGHTS + REINS

Zipcar

K.I.S.S.
(Keep It Simple, Stupid)

CLIENT
Zipcar, Inc.

ART DIRECTOR
Melanie Space

Zipcar is a fun company. I like the concept of sharing a car. I just hope the guy before me didn't step in dog poop and wipe it on the carpet.

But enough about that. They needed some simple icons to tell customers what to do: Join, Reserve, Unlock, and Drive. I explored several ideas, but the more complicated the drawing, the less impact it had. Clearly, a lot of these concepts have so much going on, you don't know what you're supposed to do. Just get a cab.

So, I scrapped those and pared it all down to simple transactions done by hand. I wish I had done that to begin with.

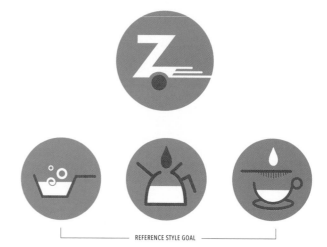

REFERENCE STYLE GOAL

Icon Exploration

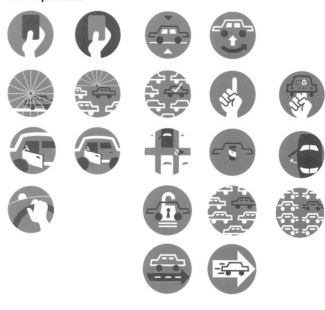

JOIN

RESERVE

UNLOCK

DRIVE

THINK, THEN JOIN

SAY YOU'LL JOIN

HAPPY TO JOIN

RESERVE

UNLOCK

DRIVE

Coca-Cola

Distilling a messy, complicated process into a palatable idea

CLIENT
Coca-Cola Company

AGENCY
Methodologie

ART DIRECTORS
Dale Hart

Trying to communicate how a product is made and distributed using icons can get a little dicey, but that's what I was hired to do for an annual report for Coca-Cola. First of all, I had to simplify the process and keep it "happy." This is Coke, after all, and no one wants to be reminded that soda is pumped full of unhealthy chemicals and sugar (particularly people like me who love Coke). I tried to connect everything and give it order—from the lab, to the factory, to the bottling and distribution, to the consumer—but they ended up going with single icons. I guess, in the end, if you're talking to shareholders, it doesn't matter.

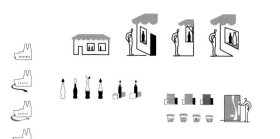

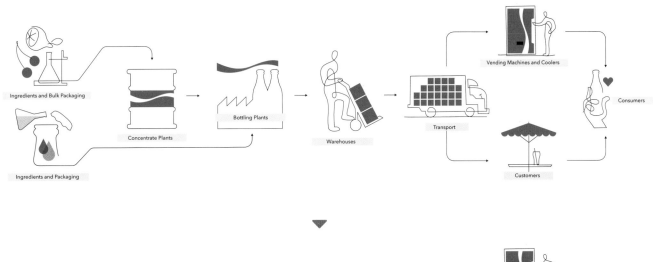

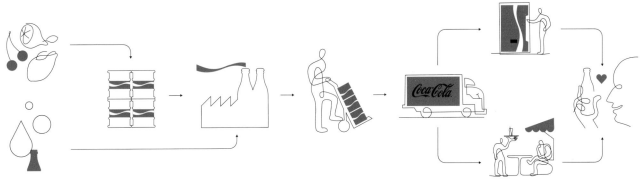

Starting with the ingredients, manufacturing, and eventually getting Coke to the consumer, this process was designed to illustrate bland information. Having worked in the beverage area for twenty-five years, I felt good working on a brand that I personally favor.

Tree Saver

Pissing off designers one owl at a time

CLIENT
Roger Black Studio, Inc.

ART DIRECTOR
Roger Black

Several years back, famed publication designer Roger Black was devising a new digital publishing platform called Tree Saver. It was intended to be a readymade template for anyone who wanted to publish an online magazine without having to hire a designer, thus pissing off a lot of designers. He asked me to come up with a logo for his paper-free publishing platform.

If an owl hoots and no one hears it, does that mean it didn't happen? Well, maybe, and in this case, yes. See all those nice owls I drew? Well, one finally passed muster, but the company went bankrupt. Good night, owl.

Because none of this stuff was used, I kept the seed and leaf idea and quickly designed a symbol that visually represented the USDA Organic badge, just for fun. The original symbol isn't readable in small sizes on packaging, which really annoys me.

SIMPLE, BALANCED   HAS BETTER MOVEMENT   HAS @ SYMBOL QUALITY

Recycling, right?
I started with a few ideas left over from Sony Green.

MNEMONIC DEVICE, OR CHARACTER THAT CHANGES/EXPANDS?

Hoot, hoot. Owls galore. Who gives a hoot?

Digicel and Avaya

Two different perspectives

Usually, when you're starting a project for a communications company, certain design elements come to mind, like radiating bars or phone icons. But they don't always work, and there isn't a one-size-fits-all for this category.

Cases in point: The work I did for Digicel and Avaya couldn't be more different in approach and execution.

CLIENT
Cliff Freeman & Partners

ART DIRECTOR
Tom Christman

Digicel, which is based in Jamaica, offers phones and service plans to its Caribbean customers, most of whom use phone cards to pay as they go. I tried several angles with this one . . . working with the name, creating phone icons, and using obvious cultural symbols. After numerous iterations, the client wanted to retain their logo, which was done in Comic Sans. So, there you go.

CLIENT
Templin Brink

ART DIRECTOR
Joel Templin

Avaya, on the other hand, was completely type-driven. The letters in the name flow so seamlessly together and create a cool graphic on their own, so I played with this idea of making the letters look like a dandelion. When the "wind" blows the delicate flower, the letters fly through the air and when they land, they form the word *Avaya*. It just worked.

The lack of bridge in the *A* helped create an icon that performed as both a wordmark and a logo.

A-M

"Every person looking at that image has to come away with the same understanding or the icon fails."

Editorial

116 Love Trumps All
120 *Real Simple* Icons
122 *International Herald Tribune*
128 Parsons The New School
130 *The Atlantic Monthly*
132 Obama
134 Comedy Central

Most people don't read anymore. We skim. We look for little nuggets of information. Editorial icons are those nuggets. They give readers a cursory glance at the content, enabling them to decide whether they want to read it or skip it. These are fun to draw because often there are so many ways to illustrate a topic or an article that it becomes a game. It can also be a test of endurance because you're often creating visual references for intangible ideas, like emotions, for instance. You also have to consider the broad audience you're communicating with. Every person looking at that image has to come away with the same understanding or the icon fails.

Another challenge with editorial projects is the timeline—it's almost always a tight turnaround. Like most illustrators, I'm better when the pressure is on. Having that ticking clock makes me think and draw fast, so I often have a lot of output. A lot of it is crap, but there's always a gem hidden in the pile. Most of my best work is for editorial projects. The stuff that didn't make the cut goes back in the Sock drawer for another time.

An Art Director's Guide to Working with Illustrators

By John Korpics, former creative director for ESPN, *Fortune*, *InStyle*, *Esquire*, *Entertainment Weekly*, and *GQ*; presently, chief of marketing, Harlem Village Academies charter network

There are roughly a trillion illustrators in the world. So how do you pick one? Here's a quick guide to how I've done it over the years. I'm not saying it's how YOU should do it (actually, it probably isn't); it's just a method that has worked for me (keep in mind that I've been fired more than once in my career, so . . . there's that).

PLAYERS LOGO

PLAYERS GOLF PARODIES
GOLF DIGEST
CREATIVE DIRECTOR KEN DELAGO
ART DIRECTOR CHLOE GALKIN

First, I look for the sweet spot between how talented you are and how much of a jerk you are. Generally, it's just not worth working with someone who is going to be a pain in the ass, no matter how clever their ideas are or how beautifully they can craft a line. There's always someone whose work may be just a micron less remarkable than yours, but who won't be all high and mighty just because they got a call to do a cover for Paul Auster's latest collection of short stories.

Second, I want to know whether you can solve MY problem, not forward your own agenda. I don't want to have to think of the really great idea that solves the problem—that's what I'm paying you to do! I'm the one with a deadline, the twenty other problems that you don't know about, and the boss who has the inspirational poster in her office of a bunch of geese flying in a V formation that says "Teamwork." So, I need to know that we are going to work together to solve MY problem.

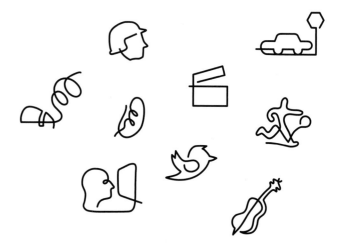

Which leads me right into. . . I need to know that you can take direction. Your amazing idea may very well be as important to modern culture as *Les Demoiselles d'Avignon* (as you have no doubt told me by now), but the illustration that I need is 2 inches (5 cm) square and it's due tomorrow. Oh, and by the way, I work for a trade magazine (in this scenario at least) about farm equipment, not the *New York* effin' *Times*, so I need you to get on board with my brand because I am focused on the 75,000 farmers who are going to see this, not the next American Illustration competition you are going to enter. Also, I'm going to need sketches and revised sketches later today, final art tomorrow, and I have $150.

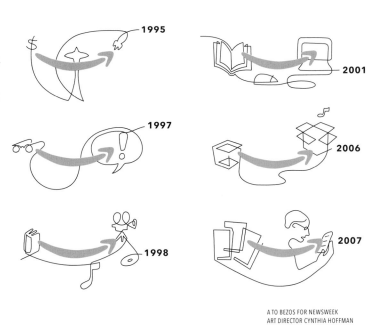

A TO BEZOS FOR NEWSWEEK
ART DIRECTOR CYNTHIA HOFFMAN

CREATIVE DIRECTOR KEN DELAGO
ART DIRECTOR CHLOE GALKIN

MASTERS LOGO

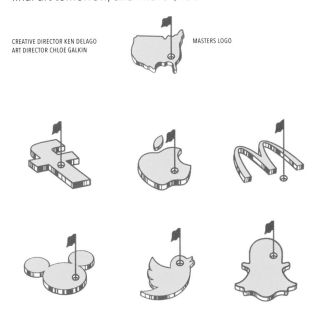

Finally, you need to be able to draw. This one may sound obvious, but honestly, there is a grand canyon of illustrators out there who can't even draw the cowboy on the matchbox. There is a real craft to this, and it takes honest-to-goodness hard work, practice, and repetition to get good at it. The more comfortable you are at drawing, the bigger the variety of ideas you will be comfortable coming up with, which means I will be the beneficiary of those ideas, not to mention that you will start to get more work. It's simple, really: the limits of your ability to draw will limit the ideas you come up with, which will in turn limit the money you will make.

I share all of this with you today not because I harbor any resentment toward the illustration community, but because I respect it so much! I love illustration and illustrators, and I feel incredibly fortunate to have been able to work with some of the best in the business over the years. The right illustrator can become a part of your brand, solve your problems, tell stories, draw you into content, make you laugh or pause or think twice. They can clarify the complex, denigrate the deplorables, eviscerate the evildoers, topple monarchs, and change the world. But there is a reason that 2 percent of the illustrators in the world get 99 percent of the work. In my opinion, it's because the 2 percent are smarter, more clever, have a point of view, can draw better, can take direction, and mostly, they aren't jerks. Mostly.

I hope this has been helpful. Oh, and Felix? He's all of that and a bag of chips.

Love Trumps All

An opportunity too good to pass up

COLLABORATORS
Thomas Fuchs
Josh Friedland

I initially illustrated a book with Thomas Fuchs in 2004, when George W. Bush was elected, called *Deconstructing Dumbo: The GOP 100*. We created 100 elephant icons in various states, such as an apple and a serpent to show how sneaky the Republicans were in getting Bush elected or the bottom half of an elephant disconnected from its brain. We had a lot of fun creating satirical images.

Fast-forward to 2015/2016, with Donald Trump running for president. Wow, what a gift! Josh Friedland and I used the same images and paired them with statements that Trump may or may not have said. See whether you can figure out which are true and which are false. It's not as easy as it looks.

1874

1976

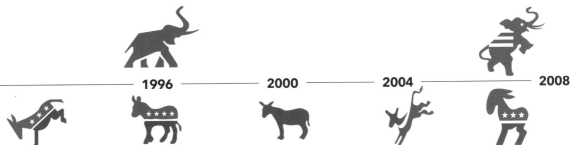

 1996 **2000** **2004** **2008**

1 The Bible ☐ True ☐ False

"I love the Bible. I love the Bible.
I'm a Protestant, I'm a Presbyterian."

2 War ☐ True ☐ False

"I'm really good at war.
I love war in a certain way, but
only when we win."

3 Education ☐ True ☐ False

"Our kids are the best students
in the world. No question. But we're gonna
have to lose Common Core."

4 Money ☐ True ☐ False

"I like money. I'm very greedy. I'm a greedy person.
I shouldn't tell you that. I've always been a greedy
person. I love money, right?"

5 Capitol Punishment ☐ True ☐ False

"We have to punish the criminals. We need
to punish. I love the death penalty, but we don't
use it enough."

6 The Middle East ☐ True ☐ False

"I love the Middle East, but it's a disaster.
A total disaster. We need to destroy ISIS or we're all
going to be eating falafel. Have you had falafel?
Trust me, you don't want falafel."

7 MSNBC ☐ True ☐ False

"Morning Joe is great. Mika loves me
too. She says negative things, but frankly, she's
attracted to me. Can't blame her."

8 Wisconsin ☐ True ☐ False

"I love Wisconsin. It's a great place."

9 New York ☐ True ☐ False

"I love New York City. Love the energy. No
other place like it. Do we need Staten Island?
Probably not. It needs to be looked at."

10 Taxes ☐ True ☐ False

"We need taxes. We have to tax. I pay.
Trust me, I pay. You know I pay. But I love
to pay as little as possible."

11 Taxes ☐ True ☐ False

"I love taxes. We have to tax people.
Have you been to the Camen Islands?
Tremendous beaches."

12 John McCain ☐ True ☐ False

"I love veterans. And prisoners of war.
The ones who escape—not the ones who get
caught—like John McCain."

13 Wildlife ☐ True ☐ False

"I love nature, but listen, I'm a city guy.
Come on. We need to look at the National Parks.
That's prime real estate. If we don't,
we're losing. Big time."

14 Suicide ☐ True ☐ False

"I love suicide. Sometimes I wish I were
dead but who would spend my money? Melania?
I'd rather kill myself than let her spend it."

15 Race ☐ True ☐ False

"People of color are lovely people. But
dangerous. We need to take a look at some things.
'Trust but verify' those people."

16 Climate Change ☐ True ☐ False

"I love climate change. It's great."

17 Veterans ☐ True ☐ False

"The VA is a scandal. It's corrupt, and what's going on
is a disgrace. And, believe me, if I win, if I become
president, that will end. I love veterans."

18 Planning ☐ True ☐ False

"It's tangible, it's solid, it's beautiful.
It's artistic, from my standpoint, and I
just love real estate."

19 Planning ☐ True ☐ False

"You can't overthink things. I loved
George Bush but he thought too much."

20 Family ☐ True ☐ False

"My family is beautiful. I love my family.
Look at Ivanka. I mean, come on. She's a
beautiful, beautiful woman. If I saw her on
Tinder, I would swipe right. Just saying."

21 Waterboarding ☐ True ☐ False

"They asked me, 'What do you think about waterboarding, Mr. Trump?' I said I love it. I love it, I think it's great."

22 Anatomy ☐ True ☐ False

"I love my hands. They're not small. Look at these hands. They're huge. Absolutely not small I tell you. You're not looking at the right angle."

23 The Party ☐ True ☐ False

"I love the Republicans but their party's a disaster, I gotta tell ya!"

24 Sin ☐ True ☐ False

"We all sin right? Sin is good. I love to sin a little bit. Just ask my three wives."

25 Incarceration ☐ True ☐ False

"I've built a lot of hotels. And they're the best in the world. The best. And you know what, we're going to build the best prisons. They're going to be tremendous. I love prisons."

26 Truth ☐ True ☐ False

"I love to hear good stories but you should never lie. I try not to lie. I've never lied. That I know of."

27 Labor ☐ True ☐ False

"Cheap labor, if you can get it, is a lovely thing. Mexico and China— they work cheap. We don't. It needs to be looked at."

28 Soda ☐ True ☐ False

"I love Coke but I also like Pepsi. I prefer Coke with a straw sometimes—*if you know what I'm talkin' about*. Coke is great."

29 Disney ☐ True ☐ False

"I love Disney. The lines, frankly, are too long. We need to do something about that. And we will. But I really love Disney."

30 E.T. ☐ True ☐ False

"I love ET. Phenomenal movie. A great, great movie. Children love it. Wonderful story. Drew Barrymore, I could do without."

31 Elderly ☐ True ☐ False

"I love the elderly. They love me. We do really, really well with the old people."

32 Shoes ☐ True ☐ False

"I love a variety of high-end shoes. I can remember when I thought some good shoes were great until I found some really great shoes."

33 Potatoes ☐ True ☐ False

"Thank you Idaho! I love your potatoes—nobody grows them better."

34 Hispanics ☐ True ☐ False

"The best taco bowls are made in Trump Tower Grill. I love Hispanics."

35 Oreos ☐ True ☐ False

"Oreos! I love Oreos; I'll never eat them again. I'll never eat them again."

36 World Peace ☐ True ☐ False

"I love world peace. But I love war too."

37 Harrison Ford ☐ True ☐ False

"I love Harrison Ford — and not just because he rents my properties."

38 The U.S.A. ☐ True ☐ False

"U.S.A. U.S.A. U.S.A. I love it!"

39 Women ☐ True ☐ False

"I respect women, I love women, I cherish women. You know, Hillary Clinton said, 'he shouldn't cherish,' well, I said, I do cherish, I love women."

40 Neil Young ☐ True ☐ False

"I love Neil Young. And he loves me! We have a great relationship."

Real Simple Icons

Simple wayfinding cues

CLIENT
RealSimple.com

CREATIVE DIRECTOR
Janet Froelich

ART DIRECTOR
Cybelle Grandjean

When Janet Froelich took over as the creative director for *Real Simple* in 2009, she revamped many of the regular columns and added new ones. She hired me to create little topical, wayfinding icons that would sit at the top of every other page.

Paul Rand once said, "Circles are the perfect shape." That didn't square with everyone, but he had a point (sorry). Over the course of ten years, my circular icons for *Real Simple* held court in a small but memorable way on nearly every page. The process was fairly rigorous and the results were not always "one line," but appropriate to the aesthetic. When the holidays rolled around, I'd do some new ones—turkey icons for Thanksgiving, caps for graduation, etc.

Over the years, any time they would need an icon, they would call and we'd knock some out. We did a couple hundred. Now that they're laid to rest, the assorted lot will circle back into the Sock drawer and will be given a reprise at another date and time.

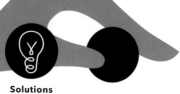

Solutions

Food

Life Lessons

Your Words

Gift Guide

International Herald Tribune

Identifying the female factor

CLIENT
New York Times

ART DIRECTOR
Kelly Doe

The *International Herald Tribune* wanted to examine where women stood in the early twenty-first century through a yearlong series of articles, columns, and multimedia reports. They wanted a visual reference for the series, so I started playing with women's likenesses. Typically, female images arrive in a one, two punch—in this case, a globe and a woman.

Of all the options presented, this was my least favorite, but after some lovin', it began to grow on me.

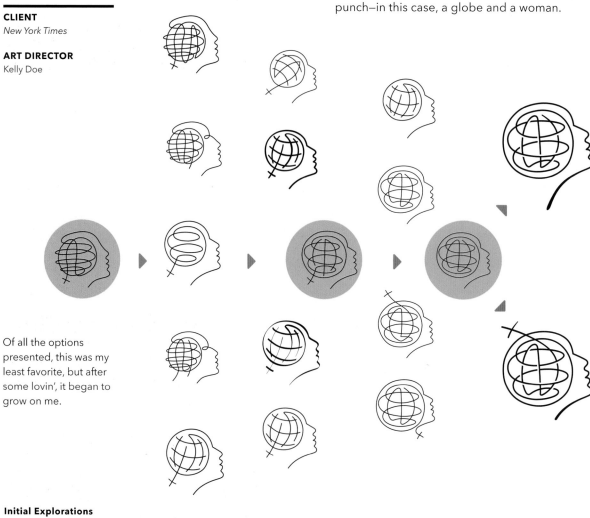

Initial Explorations

1   2   3   4   5   6   7   8

The light refracts from the lines in a way that makes the eye look at it so you see the image without getting clogged up. There are a lot of lines that intersect. Do you draw them from the bottom or the top? Does it make sense? A lot of it is just an aesthetic thing, where you have to toy with it in order to see what works.

The hardest part was gauging how thick the stroke should be and what parts of the line would be better served in the back or front. I broke some rules with this that I don't usually employ. In the end, the face is tilted, and I think it works.

The line weight and balance of the image needed to be sifted through at micro and macro levels in order to give it the right feel. Size is always an issue.

Illustrating the Many Voices of the *New York Times* Op-Ed Page

By Brian Rea, former art director, *New York Times* Op-Ed Page

During my time working as art director for the op-ed page at the *New York Times*, I had the opportunity to commission Felix for many illustration projects. He produced op-ed illustrations that ran on the opinion page as well as "letters pieces"—images that ran alongside a letter or group of letters on the letters to the editor page.

To some artists, creating illustrations for the letters section was less glamorous than producing work for the op-ed page because the letters pieces were the smaller image on the spread (often 2 × 2.5 inches [5 × 6 cm]). However, Felix loved working on them and his work was ideally suited for the format—striking graphic images with incredibly sharp ideas, often with a twist.

Most artists that I commissioned each day would submit two to four ideas—Felix would submit a page full of possible solutions. His output for effective ideas was incredible, and I came to rely on him for projects with ridiculously tight turnaround times, as well as those challenging topics that required imagery with intelligence, sensitivity, and impact.

The thing I loved about working with Felix is that he looked at illustration more like collaboration, as if he were problem solving WITH the art director rather than working FOR an art director. His goals were the same as mine: aim to put the

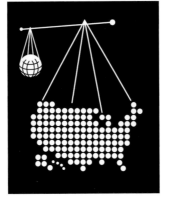

IMMI
GRRRR
ATION

(Hint: Answers to Come)

smartest, strongest piece on the page. So any discussion of revisions or adjustments he clearly understood, and he'd simply work around the idea further. On any of his projects, if you follow Felix's sketches in order of development, you can see how he was thinking about each illustration problem—how he turned the ideas over, inside out, subtracting unnecessary elements, adding in critical information, finessing, and fine-tuning—until all that was left was a gem of a solution that fit beautifully in a 2-inch (5 cm) space.

Editor's note: It's all fun and games in the op-ed section, but clearly, Rea didn't do a book with Felix.

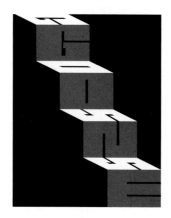

War Torn

One such topic was a piece on post-traumatic stress disorder (PTSD) in soldiers returning from war. I recall some discussion on his initial ideas—they were strong graphically, but perhaps lacking the human or emotional component. So, I went back to Felix and discussed the concerns. He understood exactly what was needed—something that not only had a strong illustrative metaphor, but also worked emotionally and of course, graphically on the page. He kept at it, carving out more and more ideas, exploring the topic a bit deeper, and using more accuracy and refinement, and focused on the posture of the soldier to suggest his state of mind. His finished idea had a quiet power on the page—not an easy thing to do with an image so small.

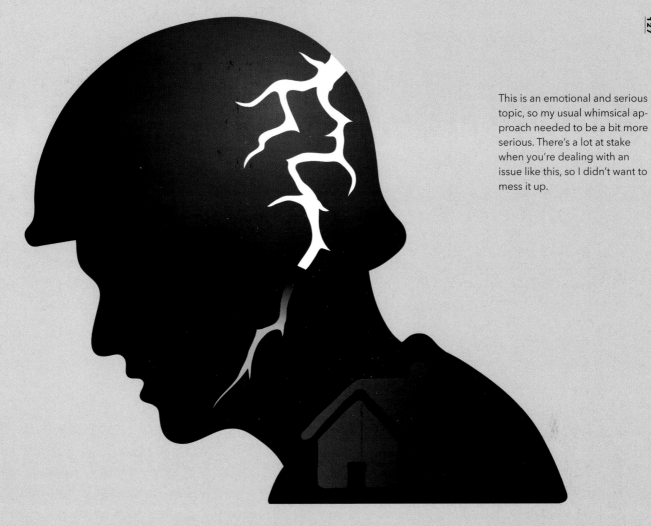

This is an emotional and serious topic, so my usual whimsical approach needed to be a bit more serious. There's a lot at stake when you're dealing with an issue like this, so I didn't want to mess it up.

Exploratory

Parsons The New School

Editorial collaborations: when two heads are better than one

OUTREACH AND VOLUNTEER RECRUITMENT

CLIENT
Parsons School of Design

COLLABORATORS
Chip Wass
Nicholas Blechman

ART DIRECTOR
Evelyn Kim

MEDIA DISCUSSIONS

SPREADING THE WORD

I collaborated with friends on two separate projects for Parsons. It's always fun to work back and forth with someone else to get a different perspective. I'll send something that's almost finished, and then they'll take it and give it a completely different look. I love when that happens and our combined styles complement each other.

ADVOCATING POLICY

Right:
Chip Wass and I made these spot illustrations for a recruitment brochure. We batted these back and forth. There are participants and actions (actions are in red). Once this was established, the game played itself.

Far right:
Every year, Parsons designs a brochure with its course offerings, and every year they hire an illustrator. Nicholas Blechman and I did these little icons and spot illustrations in 2001. I always learn something from collaborating with other artists and you can see the hybrid nature of the work. I can also see some Richard McGuire influence here—a brilliant artists who was my neighbor at the time.

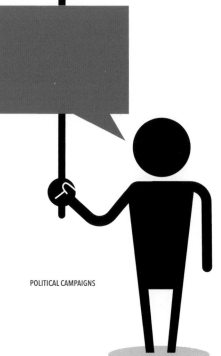

POLITICAL CAMPAIGNS

CONTINUING ED

PAINTING	DESIGN	INTERIOR DESIGN	COMPUTER DESIGN	PHOTOGRAPHY	FASHION DESIGN	CONTINUING EDUCATION

Parsons School of Design
Office of Continuing Education
66 Fifth Avenue
New York, NY 10011

Periodicals Rate
PAID
New York, New York
Permit No. 760-830

Parsons

continuing education
volume 18 number **5** fall 2001

→ ART AND DESIGN

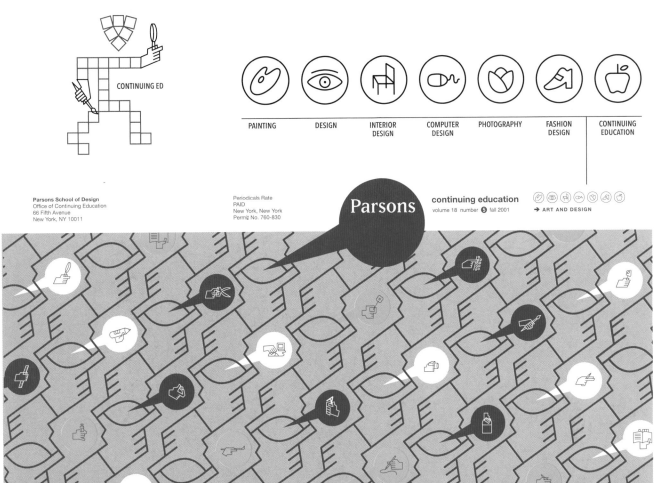

New School University
Parsons School of Design

FASHION DESIGN

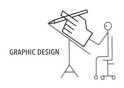

GRAPHIC DESIGN

PRE-COLLEGE ACADEMY

DIGITAL DESIGN

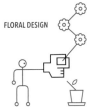

FLORAL DESIGN

The Atlantic Monthly

Visual navigation device for readers

CLIENT
The Atlantic Monthly

CREATIVE DIRECTOR
Michael Bierut

ART DIRECTOR
Jason Treat

As part of the redesign of *The Atlantic* many years ago, art director Jason Treat hired me to create little wayfinding icons for the table of contents to represent the different sections of the magazine. Stylistically, we wanted a linear connection with the icons. I suggested using a little color–the red–to create a cohesive look. These needed to be tactile, not trendy, as they would be in use for a long time . . . ten years, I believe.

Round 1

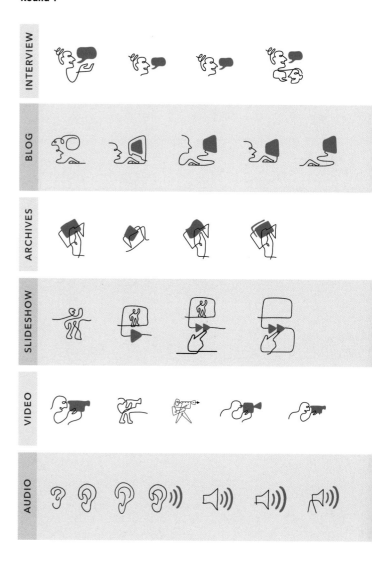

Interview Icon

When I did this icon, I envisioned a woman with a bun. Turns out, I was way ahead of my time. Nowadays, this could be a dude with a man-bun.

Round 2	Round 3	Round 4	Final

Obama

Bring on the hope . . . we need it now more than ever

CLIENT
Self-initiated

Obey, Obama, Obeyma . . . In 2008, we were all so full of hope, we bled optimism. . . at least liberals did. We were all so damn proud of ourselves for voting for our first African-American president, and you just couldn't wipe the grins off our smug faces. Shepard Fairey's Hope campaign posters were celebrated, stolen, and copied.

In my own celebratory way, I jumped on the bandwagon. This little self-initiated image led to some great things in 2008 and 2009. It was printed on posters and stickers for fundraisers pre-election and then published in *Design for Obama: Posters for Change* by Steven Heller, Aaron Perry-Zucker, and Spike Lee. It features hundreds of images submitted by designers and artists. As a result of the book, I was invited to speak and teach a workshop in Ecuador, where I met the U.S. ambassador and a lot of interesting students. Sometimes, it pays to play.

I had to distill facial features and line thicknesses to accommodate sticker production.

Trying to bridge the gap between André the Giant and Obama was a game in and of itself.

Comedy Central

A graphic see-section

CLIENT
Self-initiated

In 2010, I saw some really bad graphics on *The Daily Show* that were promoting a rally Jon Stewart and Stephen Colbert were doing called the "Rally to Restore Sanity and/or Fear." Basically, they were responding to an earlier event hosted by conservative talk show personality Glenn Beck called "Restoring Honor." Designer Neal Aspinall created a nice poster for the Beck event that relied heavily on a Michael Schwab aesthetic.

On the other hand, the graphics for the Stewart/Colbert rally were atrocious. They were so bad I thought it was a joke. The portraits were awful, and it looked like an intern created them. They even copied the steps from Beck's poster. It didn't work.

So, I redrew it and put it up on my website. In this case, aesthetics trumped concept because the concept was to parody Beck. But here's the thing: nobody gives a sh*t. Beck's rally was months before, and if you're going to parody something, make it actually mean something.

Above:
Comedy Central's original logo and inspiration from Glenn Beck's rally poster. Check out the weird gray halftone and blue containment line. It's a mess.

TEAM**SANITY**

TEAM**FEAR**

RALLY TO

RESTORE SANITY

★ 10.30.10 WASHINGTON, D.C. ★

I'M WITH
SANITY

SANITY

SAY HELLO TO
SWEETNESS

MARCH TO

KEEP FEAR ALIVE!

★ 10.30.10 WASHINGTON, D.C. ★

FEAR

"You can't be too clever when it comes to wayfinding because it will just lead to confusion."

Wayfinding

138 California State Parks

142 Bronx River Alliance

146 *New York Times*
Science Section

152 A Parody of
Wayfinding Icons

Wayfinding icons are designed to help people get from point A to point B with as little confusion as possible. They are often universal symbols that anyone in any language or culture can seamlessly understand. Think of the male and female icons you see on restroom doors. Easy, right? Sometimes the easiest solutions are the hardest to arrive at. You can't be too clever when it comes to wayfinding because it will just lead to confusion. Wayfinding icons can be anything, really—animals, to identify species at a zoo or park; people doing things, such as walking, working, embracing; or symbols, like a cross to show a railroad crossing, etc. The simpler, the better to send you on your way.

California State Parks

When the call of the wild falls on deaf ears

CLIENT
AdamsMorioka, Inc.

ART DIRECTORS
Sean Adams
Noreen Morioka

Branding a state park is a lot of fun, or at least it could be if you weren't working with a government agency for approval. AdamsMorioka hired me to create a unified wayfinding system for California State Parks. The current brand elements were all over the place with different typefaces and illustration styles. It's like a branding case study of what NOT to do.

   I drew all kinds of animals for this, including mountain lions, turtles, quail, and squirrels, in a way that unified the brand. There were also practical implications: because these physical signs would be subject to harsh weather conditions, we wanted them replicated in iron signage, which also wouldn't obstruct the nature of the landscape.

STAY CONNECTED SANTA MONICA

Noreen sent me silhouettes and applications of different animal icons, which I then translated into my linear style for the signs.

SANTA
MONICA
MOUNTAINS

Taking my illustration style and integrating it into the typography meant using it in a way that felt like Art Deco meeting mid-century.

TAQUETEASYBRA

THIS WAY TO WAVES   THIS WAY TO TRAILS   BE NICE TO SQUIRRELS   LIONS ROCK BRAH   PARK YOUR PRIUS

Bronx River Alliance

The annual showcase for bored designers who want to do some pro bono stuff

CLIENT
DesigNYC

PROJECT LEADER
Steven Heller

CO-DESIGNER
Thomas Vasquez

DesigNYC is a grassroots organization founded by design leaders who wanted to create social change in the city by volunteering their design services. I was lured in to create branding and signage for the City of New York Parks and Recreation—notably, the Bronx River Alliance. Steven Heller was my cheerleader and guide in this venture.

I almost felt like a park volunteer. I had to spend hours there learning about different kinds of fish. It took months and mountains of revisions and meetings. The coalitions of people who make these decisions are also volunteers, and I learned that they all felt like they needed to assert their opinions. They argued about the types of fish I drew and whether it looked like a catfish versus a bullfish. It resulted in a lot of wasted time and energy.

This is the original mark. They didn't ask me to redesign it, but I felt it needed to happen, given that it didn't reduce well and was hard to read.

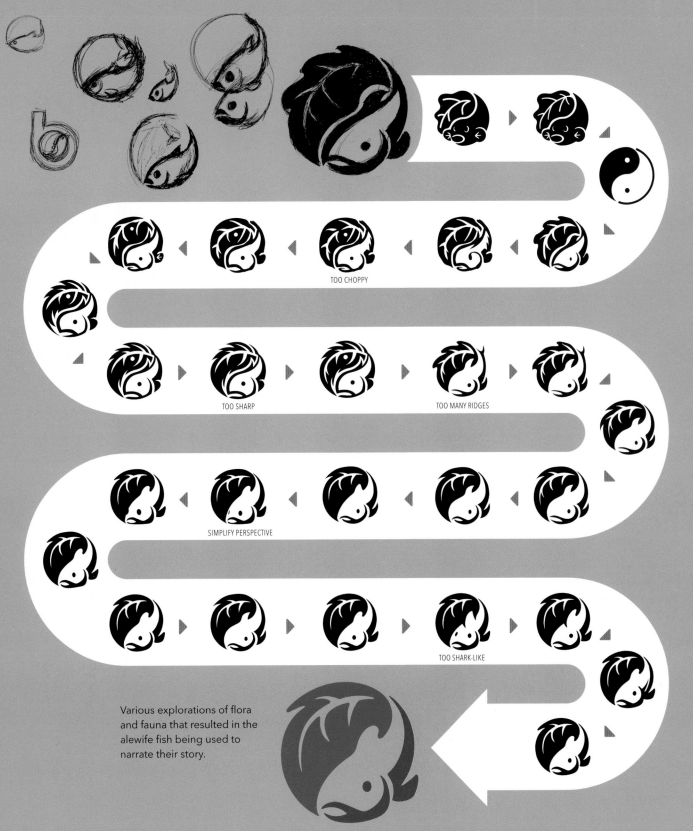

TOO CHOPPY

TOO SHARP

TOO MANY RIDGES

SIMPLIFY PERSPECTIVE

TOO SHARK-LIKE

Various explorations of flora and fauna that resulted in the alewife fish being used to narrate their story.

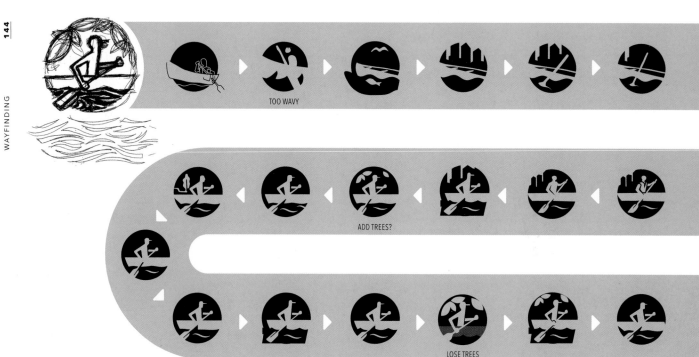

TOO WAVY

ADD TREES?

LOSE TREES

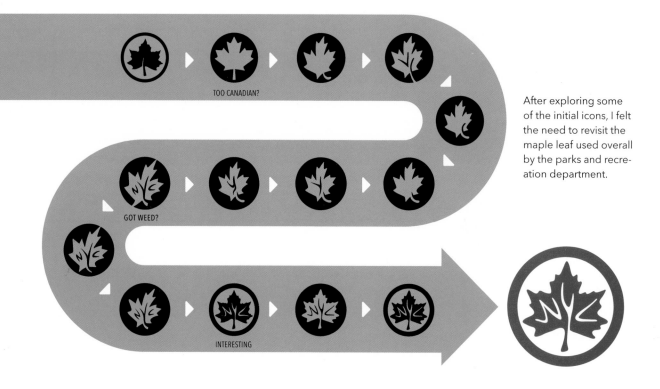

TOO CANADIAN?

GOT WEED?

INTERESTING

After exploring some of the initial icons, I felt the need to revisit the maple leaf used overall by the parks and recreation department.

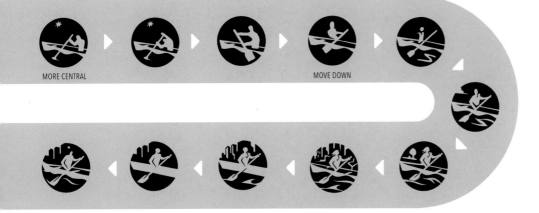

MORE CENTRAL

MOVE DOWN

bronx river alliance

bronx river flotilla

ADD CITYSCAPE?

I distilled the elements of the cityscape, water, and rower in the circular shape to complement the logo.

parks and recreation

river blueway

river greenway

I also blew out the BlueWay and GreenWay logos, which belonged in their branding program.

BR🐟NX
river alliance

BR🍁NX
river flotilla

New York Times Science Section

Developing a visual language for nonvisual ideas

CLIENT
New York Times

ART DIRECTOR
Kelly Doe

COLLABORATOR
Jerry Kuyper

Communicating ideas that don't necessarily correlate to a form or an image is always tricky and very sub-jective. People have their own ideas of what certain terms mean to them. Aging, Longevity, Optimism, Pregnan-cy, Hazards, Risks, Filters, etc.–the task of designing images for these partic-ularly tough and vague subjects was daunting. A mix of metaphors, type, numbers, and scientific equations seemed appropriate, but not initially. I fumbled around for a few days before I got a handle on it.

I was helped along by fellow designer/collaborator Jerry Kuyper, who showed me the flat square screen (bottom middle, opposite page). From there on, it was just a matter of paring down various ingredients and building out the language in a way that felt scientific. Everything in this system is reliant on 45-degree angles.

Row 1: Aging, Childbirth, Nutrition, Patterns
Row 2: Awareness, Childhood, Prognosis, Prevention
Row 3: Disparities, Exercise, Perceptions, Regimens
Row 4: Hazards, Longevity, Risks, Safety
Row 5: Mental Health, Nostrums, Screening, Symptoms

I felt a headless pregnant woman would go over well, but it looks like she's swallowed a beachball.

This crosswalk symbol wasn't used or even shown, but it has a certain look and feel that I recalled and used later for something else.

The subtle shadow under the nail works in this calendar, but calendars themselves are outdated.

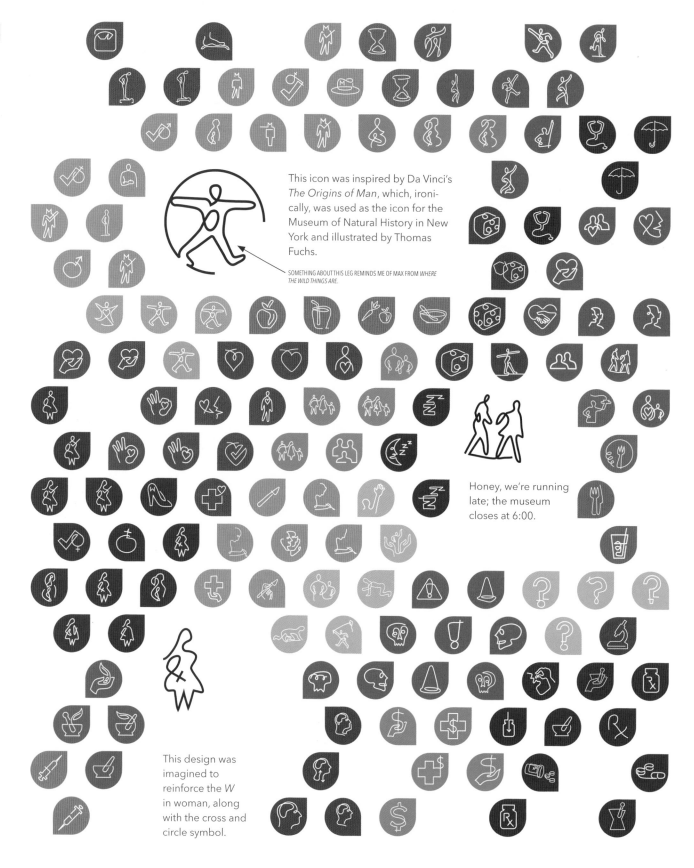

This icon was inspired by Da Vinci's *The Origins of Man*, which, ironically, was used as the icon for the Museum of Natural History in New York and illustrated by Thomas Fuchs.

SOMETHING ABOUT THIS LEG REMINDS ME OF MAX FROM *WHERE THE WILD THINGS ARE.*

Honey, we're running late; the museum closes at 6:00.

This design was imagined to reinforce the *W* in woman, along with the cross and circle symbol.

Relationships

I initially tried this icon with a hands-off approach, but he needed some lovin'.

Parenting/Family

This one was a refurb. I took some old ideas for family, redrew them in a way that distilled the information, then, last minute, went for the scratch. I'm the only one who saw the humor in it.

Row 1:
Fitness, Food, Dieting/Weight, Nutrition, Relationships

Row 2:
Parenting/Family, Mind, Sleep, Body, Cancer

Row 3:
Heart, Well Man, Well Woman, Well Child, Pregnancy

Row 4:
Aging, Risks, Ask Well, Alternative Medicine, Doctors

Row 5:
Drugs, Vaccinations, Hazards, Patient Money, Prevention

SHANGHAI

SYDNEY

TORONTO

STOCKHOLM

SANTIAGO

OSLO

SEYKJAVIK

SAN JOSE

AREQIUIPA

NEW YORK

PARIS

HELSINKI

COPENHAGEN

TAIPEI

LISBON

HONG KONG

ROME

MEXICO CITY

WARSAW

MADRID

MOSCOW

PRAGUE

BANGKOK

JERUSALEM

TANGIER

TOKYO

AMSTERDAM

LONDON

EVIAN

SAN FRANCISCO

MUNICH

COLOMBO

QUITO

BEIJING

LIMA

TBLISI

RENACA

DUBAI

BUENOS AIRES

ULAN BATOR

DUBLIN

CAPETOWN

Men at Work

Felix Sockwell

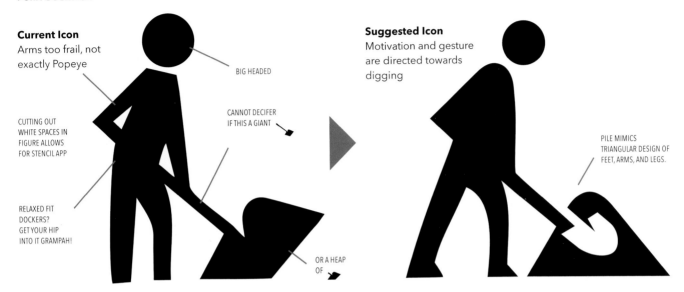

Current Icon
Arms too frail, not exactly Popeye

BIG HEADED

CANNOT DECIFER IF THIS A GIANT

CUTTING OUT WHITE SPACES IN FIGURE ALLOWS FOR STENCIL APP

RELAXED FIT DOCKERS? GET YOUR HIP INTO IT GRAMPAH!

OR A HEAP OF

Suggested Icon
Motivation and gesture are directed towards digging

PILE MIMICS TRIANGULAR DESIGN OF FEET, ARMS, AND LEGS.

One of the first things you notice when you go through airports are the wayfinding icons. Every region has subtle differences, and you get a sense of how they see themselves and how they function as a society.

Working men icons are no different. As you can see on the left, there are many scenarios depicting workers holding shovels and digging. Even the pile sizes are different. The guy in Beijing has to work three times as hard as the rest, and his shovel handle looks like it's bending under pressure. The guy in Moscow looks like Gumby, and Mr. Santiago could be busting a move. San Francisco's icon appears to be wearing a skirt and boots, so the girl can go directly from her city job to the bar for happy hour.

Seriously, though, the working man icons in the United States lack detail. There is no clear distinction between the shovel and the mound of dirt. For all we know, the San Francisco person could be getting ready to lift her umbrella over her head, and you can't tell what the guy in New York is doing. Is he raking leaves, playing golf, or shoveling snow? I did my own little version, above, to illustrate better movement and clearly distinguish the shovel in the pile. Easy peasy. Then again, these icons are so ubiquitous, does it even matter?

A Parody of Wayfinding Icons

Wayfinding icons are usually pretty serious business. They have to be instantly recognizable and straightforward so viewers know what they are supposed to do or where they're supposed to be. Some icons are so ubiquitous that they are inherently part of the visual lexicon (see page 150, Man at Work images). I took liberties with these associations and gave them a new meaning for two different projects.

Playing with a creative grading system

CLIENT
Social Design Network

This is a series of icons for a grading system to evaluate creative work. Following a series of prompts from terrible to genius, I created different scenarios for each term. Hey, folks, these icons depict the way I actually feel about my own work sometimes . . . you know, when you're slumped over the drawing board ready to bang your head against your desk? Yeah, it's there.

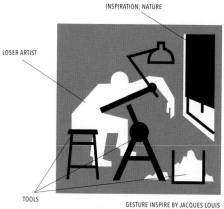

INSPIRATION; NATURE

LOSER ARTIST

TOOLS

GESTURE INSPIRE BY JACQUES LOUIS DAVID, LA MORT DE MARAT

Years ago, **Social Design Network** asked for an iconic rating system for users to grade work. I took a pass at it, failed, and used some of the thinking for a coffee table book for HBO's Entourage.

STANDS OUT   WORKS   TIRED   RETIRED

WORN OUT   KILL ME NOW

SUCKS   RETIRED   TIRED   WORKS   GENIUS

TERRIBLE   TIRED   WEAK   WORKS   INSPIRED

INSPIRED   OUTSTANDING   WORKS   SNORESVILLE   FUDDA-BIRDS

HBO's *Entourage* coffee table book

CLIENT
Ph.D

ART DIRECTOR
Mick Hodgson

This show was about a famous actor and his buddies and the shenanigans they would get into as single guys—playing video games, partying at nightclubs, cruising for chicks, banging chicks, avoiding chicks they've banged, etc. I took a tongue-in-cheek approach to this using common iconography for a coffee table book about the show.

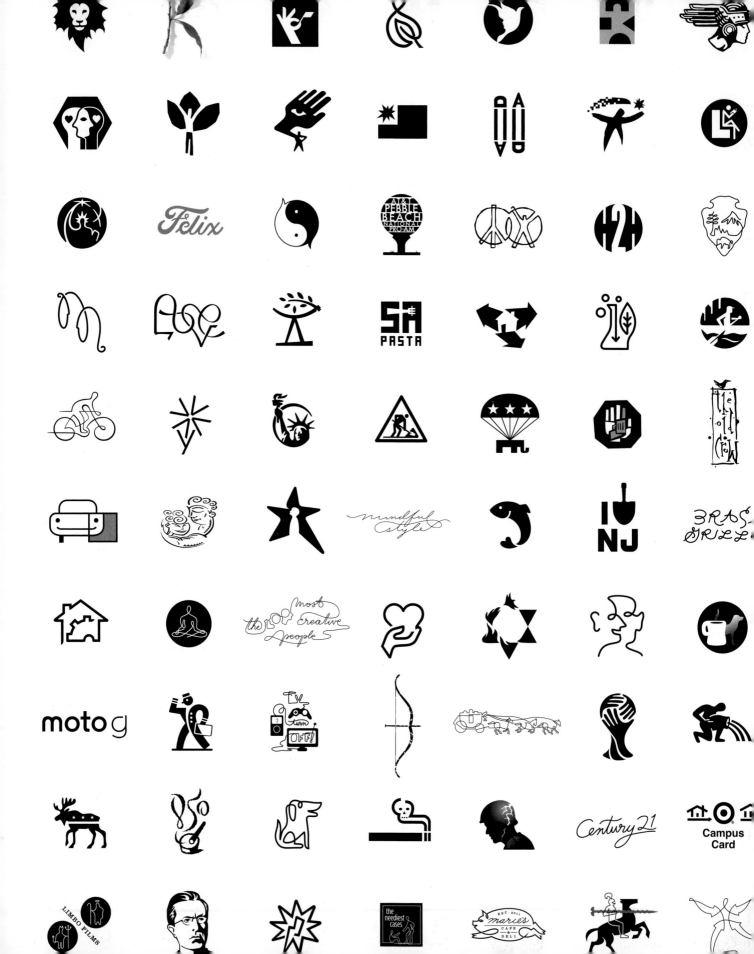

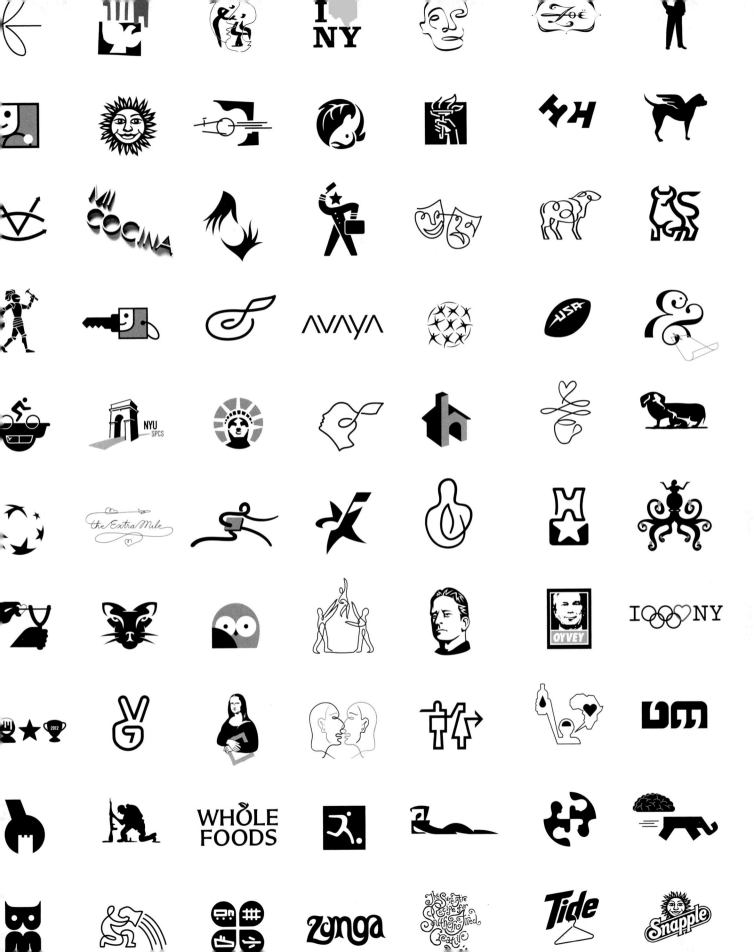

About the Authors

Felix Sockwell is an artist, graphic designer, and art director who specializes in the creation of logos, icons and icon systems, murals, and animations. He's worked with many high-profile brands, designers, and art directors, and helped develop the GUI (graphic user interface) for the *New York Times'* first iPhone app. He lives in Maplewood, New Jersey. See more of his work at www.felixsockwell.com

Emily Potts has been a writer and editor in the design industry for more than 20 years. Currently, she is an independent writer working for a variety of clients in the design industry. She lives in Peoria, Illinois. www.emilyjpotts.com

For 33 years, **Steven Heller** was an art director at the *New York Times*, and for almost 30 of those years with the *New York Times* Book Review. Currently, he is co-chair of the MFA Designer as Author Department, School of Visual Arts for New Programs, and writes the Visuals column for the *New York Times* Book Review. He was the recipient of the Smithsonian Cooper-Hewitt, National Design Museum's 2011 Design Mind Award. He is author, co-author, and editor of over 100 books on design and popular culture, and also writes The Daily Heller blog (imprint. printmag.com/daily-heller). He lives in New York City. Visit him online at www.hellerbooks.com

Index

A

AdamsMorioka, Inc., 138–141
Adams, Sean, 138
Amdahl, Kyle, 66
Amplify, 28–31
Apple, 20–23, 52–53
Aspinall, Neal, 134
The Atlantic Monthly, 130-131
AT&T, 26–27
Avaya, 109

B

Barkai, Maya, 8
Barry, Ben, 54
Bass, Saul, 26
Beckeraa, Cindy, 68
Beck, Glenn, 134
Berlin, Kim, 40
Bierut, Michael, 30, 50, 96, 130
Black, Roger, 106–107
Blechman, Nicholas, 128–129
Boms, Scott, 54
Branding icons
    Apple, 52–53
    Avaya, 109
    Broadway.com, 84–85
    Coca-Cola Company, 104–105
    Digicel, 108
    Dunkin' Donuts, 70–71
    Facebook, 54–59
    FIFA World Cup Logo, 86–87
    Goodwill, 92–93
    Hotels.com, 98–99
    H2H Sports, 88–89
    iHeartRadio, 64–65
    Liberty Mutual, 40–45
    Merrill Lynch, 68–69
    Monopoly, 38–39
    National Campaign Against Youth
      Violence, 72–73
    National Quality Center, 36–37
    New Directions Publishing, 62
    New York City Olympics Bid, 78–79
    Royal Shakespeare Company, 94–95

Snapple, 90–91
Sony, 66–67
Starwood Hotels, 98–99
Tree Saver, 106–107
United States Holocaust Memorial
    Museum, 80–83
Verizon, 96–97
Wells Fargo, 100–101
"Yogurt Company," 50–51
Zipcar, Inc., 102–103
Zynga, 46–49
Broadway.com, 84–85
Bronx River Alliance, 142–145
Bush, George W., 116

C

California State Parks, 138–141
Chang, Sung, 24
Christman, Tom, 90, 108
Chwast, Seymour, 8–9
Clients
    AdamsMorioka, Inc., 138–141
    Apple, 20–23, 52–53
    The Atlantic Monthly, 130–131
    "Client in Kansas," 92–93
    Cliff Freeman & Partners, 90–91, 108
    Coca-Cola Company, 104–105
    Co-collective (Co:), 28–31
    COLLINS, 78–79
    DesigNYC, 142–145
    Facebook, 54–59
    FCB, 72–73
    Hasbro, 38–39
    iHeartMedia, 64–65
    Hotels.com, 98–99
    iN DEMAND, 88–89
    Interbrand, 26–27
    New Directions Publishing, 62
    New York Times, 16–19, 122–123,
      124–127, 146–149
    Odopod, 46–49
    Ogilvy & Mather, 24–25
    Parsons School of Design, 128–129

Pentagram, 50–51, 96–97
Ph.D, 153
RealSimple.com, 120–121
Roger Black Studio, Inc., 106–107
Royal Shakespeare Company, 94–95
Sagmeister Inc., 36–37
Social Design Network, 152
Sony, 66–67
Starwood Hotels, 98–99
The Sterling Group, 40–45
Templin Brink, 72–73, 109
Time Inc., 68–69
United States Holocaust Memorial
    Museum, 80–83
Verizon, 30, 96–97
Wells Fargo, 100–101
Zipcar, Inc., 102–103
Cliff Freeman & Partners, 90–91, 108
Clifford, Graham, 28
Coca-Cola Company, 104–105
Co-collective (Co:), 28–31
Colbert, Stephen, 134–135
COLLINS, 78–79
Collins, Brian, 78
Comedy Central, 134–135
Cook, Roger, 8–9
Cooper, Jay, 84
Corral, Rodrigo, 62

D

The Daily Show, 134–135
Darling, Brian, 78
Deconstructing Dumbo: The GOP 100
    (Thomas Fuchs and Felix Sockwell),
    116–117
Dejanosi, Alex, 100
DeLago, Ken, 115
DesigNYC, 142–145
Digicel, 108
Doe, Kelly, 122, 146
Dolan, Guthrie, 46
Dunkin' Donuts, 70–71

E

Editorial icons
    The Atlantic Monthly, 130-131
    Comedy Central, 134-135
    International Herald Tribune,
        122-123
    Love Trumps All, 116-119
    Obama, 132-133
    Parsons School of Design, 128-129
    RealSimple.com, 120-121
Entourage coffee table book, 153
Ernstberger, Matthias, 36
Experimental projects
    Amplify, 28-31
    Apple, 52-53
    Bronx River Alliance, 142-145
    Comedy Central, 134-135
    Dunkin' Donuts, 70-71
    Facebook, 54-59
    FIFA World Cup Logo, 86-87
    Merrill Lynch, 68-69
    New York City Olympics bid, 78-79
    Obama, 132-133
    Royal Shakespeare Company, 94-95
    Snapple, 90-91
    Tree Saver, 106-107
    Wells Fargo, 100-101
    Zynga, 46-49

F

Facebook, 54-59
Fairey, Shepard, 132
Favorite projects
    The Atlantic Monthly, 130-131
    Coca-Cola Company, 104-105
    Comedy Central, 134-135
    Entourage coffee table book, 153
    FIFA World Cup Logo, 86-87
    Love Trumps All, 116-119
    Obama, 132-133
    Parsons School of Design, 128-129
    RealSimple.com, 120-121
    Social Design Network, 152
Fay, Aron, 96
FCB, 72-73

Festino, Robert, 82
FIFA World Cup Logo, 86-87
Fili, Louise, 99
Friedland, Josh, 116-119
Froelich, Janet, 120
Fuchs, Thomas, 80, 88-89, 92-93,
    116-119

G

Galkin, Chloe, 114, 115
Gardner, Bill, 32-33
Gardner Design, 32
Geismar, Thomas, 8-9
Glaser, Milton, 8, 9, 64, 74, 79
Glaubermany, Barbara, 24
Goodwill, 92-93
Grandjean, Cybelle, 120

H

H2H Sports, 88-89
Harak, Rudolph de, 8-9
Hart, Dale, 104
Hasbro, 38-39
HBO, 153
Heller, Steven, 7-9, 132, 142
Henghes, Heinz, 62
Higgins, Josh, 54
Hodgson, Mick, 153
Hoffman, Cynthia, 115
Hotels.com, 98-99

I

iHeartMedia, 64-65
iHeartRadio, 64-65
iN DEMAND, 88-89
Interbrand, 26-27
Interactive icons
    Amplify, 28-31
    AT&T, 26-27
    iTunes, 20-23
    New York Times app icons, 16-19
    Yahoo!, 24-25
International Herald Tribune, 122-123
iPhone *New York Times* app icons, 16-19
iTunes, 20-23

J

Johnson, Erik T., 72-73, 98

K

Key Brand Entertainment, 84
Killed projects
    Apple, 52-53
    Avaya, 109
    California State Parks, 138-141
    Digicel, 108
    Goodwill, 92-93
    Hotels.com, 98-99
    H2H Sports, 88-89
    iTunes, 20-23
    Liberty Mutual, 40-45
    Monopoly, 38-39
    New York City Olympics bid, 78-79
    Royal Shakespeare Company, 94-95
    Sony, 66-67
    Starwood Hotels, 98-99
    Tree Saver, 106-107
    United States Holocaust Memorial
        Museum, 80-83
    Verizon, 96-97
    Wells Fargo, 100-101
    Yahoo!, 24-25
    "Yogurt Company," 50-51
    Zynga, 46-49
Kim, Evelyn, 128
Klenart, Josh, 64
Korpics, John, 114-115
Kuyper, Jerry, 26, 146-149

L

Lees, John, 8-9
Lee, Spike, 132
Liberty Mutual, 40-45
LogoLounge, 32
Love Trumps All, 116-119

M

Marianek, Joe, 50, 52
Masaru, Katsumi, 9
Matousek, Abby, 96
McClelland, Jeff, 90

McGuire, Richard, 128
Men at Work, 150-151
Merrill Lynch, 68-69
Methodologie, 104-105
Millman, Debbie, 40
Monopoly, 38-39
Montague, Ty, 28
Morioka, Noreen, 138, 140

N

National Campaign Against Youth
    Violence, 72-73
National Quality Center, 36-37
Neurath, Otto, 6, 7, 9
New Directions Publishing, 62
New York City, 78-79
New York Times
        app icons, 16-19
        International Herald Tribune,
            122-123
        Op-Ed Page, 124-127
        Science section, 146-149
Niemann, Christoph, 90-91

O

Obama, 132-133
Obama: Posters for Change (Steven
    Heller, Aaron Perry-Zucker, and Spike
    Lee), 132
Odopod, 46-49
Ogilvy & Mather, 24-25
Olympic Games, 9, 78-79

P

Parsons School of Design, 128-129
Pentagram, 50-51, 96-97
Perry-Zucker, Aaron, 132
Ph.D, 153
post-traumatic stress disorder
    (PTSD), 127

R

Rea, Brian, 124-127
RealSimple.com, 120-121

Roger Black Studio, Inc., 106-107
Royal Shakespeare Company, 94-95

S

Sagmeister Inc., 36-37
Sagmeister, Stefan, 36, 80
Sainato, Vinny, 84
Salame, Joe, 92
Scher, Paula, 80, 82
Schwab, Michael, 134
Self-initiated projects
        Comedy Central, 134-135
        Dunkin' Donuts, 70-71
        FIFA World Cup Logo, 86-87
        Obama, 132-133
Serino Coyne, 84-85
Shanosky, Don, 8-9
Snapple, 90-91
Social Design Network, 152
Sony, 66-67
Space, Melanie, 102
Starwood Hotels, 98-99
The Sterling Group, 40-45
Stewart, Jon, 134-135
Stout, Craig, 26

T

Taylor, Jason, 38
Templin Brink, 72-73, 109
Templin, Joel, 72, 109
Time Inc., 68-69
Treat, Jason, 130
Tree Saver, 106-107
Trump, Donald, 116, 118-119
Tutino, Carolyn, 16

U

United States Holocaust Memorial
    Museum, 80-83
Upcycled projects
        Apple, 52-53
        AT&T, 26-27
        Broadway.com, 84-85
        Facebook, 54-59

Hotels.com, 98-99
Merrill Lynch, 68-69
National Campaign Against Youth
    Violence, 72-73
National Quality Center, 36-37
New Directions Publishing, 62
New York Times Science section,
    146-149
Starwood Hotels, 98-99
Tree Saver, 106-107
Verizon, 96-97

V

Vasquez, Thomas, 98, 142-145
Verizon, 30, 96-97
Victore, James, 92-93
Vignelli, Massimo, 8-9
Vinh, Khoi, 16

W

Wass, Chip, 128-129
Wayfinding icons
        Bronx River Alliance, 142-145
        California State Parks, 138-141
        Entourage coffee table book, 153
        New York Times Science section,
            146-149
        Social Design Network, 152
Wells Fargo, 100-101
Willems, Michelle, 84
Williams, Andy, 94

Y

Yahoo!, 24-25
"Yogurt Company," 50-51

Z

Zipcar, Inc., 102-103
Zwerner, Jeff, 20
Zynga, 46-49